Social Development Experiences in China

This book series brings together the latest research results of Chinese sociologists to summarize and analyse the process, mechanism and experiences of China's social development since the economic system reform. The analyses are tackled by looking into seven inter-relationships that are most often discussed among sociologists in observing the social transition in China: the relationship between the state and society; the relationship between the state and market; the relationship between the state and peasants, the relationship between the central and local governments; the relationship between government and enterprises; the relationship between urban and rural areas; the relationship between labour and capital.

More information about this series at http://www.springer.com/series/15691

Feizhou Zhou · Mingzhi Tan

Relationship between the Central Government and Local Governments of Contemporary China

中国社会科学出版社
CHINA SOCIAL SCIENCES PRESS

Springer

Feizhou Zhou
Peking University
Beijing
China

Mingzhi Tan
Land Renovation Center
Beijing
China

Translated by Xueping Shao

ISSN 2520-1557 ISSN 2520-1565 (electronic)
Social Development Experiences in China
ISBN 978-981-13-5125-9 ISBN 978-981-10-4388-8 (eBook)
https://doi.org/10.1007/978-981-10-4388-8

Jointly published with China Social Sciences Press, Beijing

The printed edition is not for sale in China Mainland. Customers from China Mainland please order the print book from China Social Sciences Press

Printed on acid-free paper

This Springer imprint is published by Springer Nature
The registered company is Springer Nature Singapore Pte Ltd.
The registered company address is: 152 Beach Road, #21-01/04 Gateway East, Singapore 189721, Singapore

The original version of the book frontmatter was revised: Co-publisher name has been updated. The erratum to the book frontmatter is available at https://doi.org/10.1007/978-981-10-4388-8_8

Contents

Chapter 1
Introduction: The Relationship Between the Central Government and Local Governments

Analyzing local government actions has always been one of the key approaches to comprehend social and economic development of contemporary China. Theoretically speaking, the understanding of government actions is mainly based on the theory of public choice and that of public finance. In simple terms, the theory of public finance regards the government as a necessary organization for providing public goods and public services. These functions of government may be dubbed "a helping hand". The theory of public choice considers the government as an organization with its own particular interests, which not only include organizational interests of the government inconsistent with the public welfare objectives of the state and the society, but also personal interests of government officials. Under certain circumstances, the government may use its own legitimate authority to skim profits from the society, which is commonly known as "extending a grabbing hand". These two opposing schools of theory, which are derived from the basic assumptions about government organizations, are both theoretically sound. In fact, the empirical question we often encounter in discussing government actions is: "which hand" the government will "extend" under particular circumstances, in other word, what factors may affect the government's way of acting?

According to the theoretical results achieved by the academia both at home and abroad, the main factors influencing the government's way of acting fall into three categories: The first category covers external factors, or the influences of social organizations and various interest groups in the society on government actions. Studying these factors, meaning to observe government actions from the "outside" of the government or focus on the relationship between the state and the society, is not the major objective of this book. The internal structures and systems of government organizations, which influence the internal interest and power distribution of government departments and supervise government officials, are factors of the second category. The third category of factors includes the macro frameworks of government organizations, namely, the central-local relations. The second and third categories of factors influencing one another strongly are major issues to be dealt with in our analysis of government actions. The central-local relations have

F. Zhou and M. Tan, *Relationship between the Central Government and Local Governments of Contemporary China*, Social Development Experiences in China,
DOI 10.1007/978-981-10-4388-8_1

multiple aspects, such as finance, personnel, military affairs and administration, and involve many complicated fields. To discuss the issues in a precise and empirical way, the authors construct their study of the central-local relations on a scrutiny of the financial relationship between the central and local governments.

1.1 Central Government and Local Governments

Judging from the perspective of finance, the functions of every government are mainly embodied in four aspects: allocating resource, distributing income, stabilizing and developing economy. Among these aspects, allocating resources and maintaining a fair distribution of income are comparatively more important. Both the economic growth and the fair distribution of income can be realized through the government's and the market's allocation of resources. These two approaches, very dissimilar though, are mutually supplementary. The government's allocation of resources is actually indispensable for achieving the aforesaid goals. In theory, whether certain resources should be allocated by the market or by the government mainly depends on the nature of the resources.

Government finance is termed as "public finance" for the reason that the government-provided resources, goods and services allocated are public in nature. Such goods and services are generally referred to as public goods and public services, which are undoubtedly termed so in relation to their private counterparts. If the levels of government were taken into account, reaching a consensus over what public services should be provided by the high-end government such as the central government and what should be provided by the local government would be difficult. In terms of pure theory, two simple conclusions, as briefed in Table 1.1, can be drawn:

The table above illustrates that services with a strong public nature are covered by the main expenditure responsibilities of the government, while services with a weak public nature may be funded by private capital. The "public nature" mentioned here is, to a great extent, related to the "externality" of goods and labor. Take urban construction for instance, the costs of constructing urban roads, bridges, green space and public transit whose public nature is the strongest are almost totally within the scope of government expenditure responsibilities. The public nature of cultural and sports venues, schools and government and public buildings is also strong, while facilities such as urban real estate, factories and companies with weak public nature are funded and operated on private capital. From the perspective of regional coverage, trans-regional public services benefiting a wide area, such as national defense, water conservancy, poverty relief and natural disaster control, are

Table 1.1 Public services of the central and local governments

	Strong public nature	Weak public nature
Trans-regional	Central government	Private
Regional	Local governments	Private

within the expenditure responsibilities of higher-end governments, while regional public services are within the expenditure responsibilities of lower-level local governments.

In the financial field, the government's scope of responsibilities for providing public goods and financial revenues are respectively referred to as the government's authority of office and authority of finance. In a state with a hierarchy of governments, governments of different levels enjoy authority of finance and office of different scopes and responsibilities. The core of inter-governmental relationships, including the relationship between the central and local governments, is the allocation of the authority of finance and office among governments of different levels.

The system of arranging the inter-governmental authority of finance and office is generally called the financial system in China. In a broad sense, the financial system is a system structure covering three major aspects, namely, the government's budget revenues (mainly from taxation), budget expenditure as well as extra-budgetary revenues and expenditure; in a narrow sense, the financial system refers to the budget management system generally covers the inter-governmental arrangement and allocation of revenues and expenditure within the budget. For example, as far as the central government is concerned, the financial system stipulates the scope, scale and expenditure patterns of tax revenues and non-tax revenues of the central government as well as how financial revenues and expenditures are allocated and shared between the central and local governments. In other word, the financial system determines the basic framework of central-local relations. As for each local government, the system not only regulates the revenues and expenditures of its own level, but also its financial relationship with the government at a level lower than it. Therefore, it can be concluded that the allocation of the authority of finance and office between the central and local governments determines the basic framework of the central-local relations.

In China, five levels of government give rise to a complicated inter-governmental financial relationship. On the whole, the overall principle for inter-governmental relationship in China is "the government at one level administering the government at a level right below it", or "one-level-down management", which means each level of government is responsible for formulating the financial system of the government at a level right below it. Therefore, there is no uniform financial system either between the central government and local governments or between various local governments. Instead, the financial system varies with the level of government. China has 34 provincial units, 333 regional and municipal units, 2862 county units, and 37,334 township units. Numerous government levels and units have complicated the financial system. However, despite their diversities, the financial systems among local governments mostly guided and influenced by the financial systems between the central and provincial governments do fall into certain patterns. This is because no matter how different they are, financial systems have to follow some principles guaranteeing the measuring standards of efficiency and equity of inter-governmental financial relationships. Generally speaking, there are three principles.

The first principle is the "symmetry" principle. One level of government should have one level of finance, that is, one level of government should be furnished with relevant budget revenues and expenditure responsibilities, and its authority of finance and office should be proportionate or symmetrical. Obviously, if the authority of office of a certain level of government far exceeds its authority of finance, this level of government will suffer from a financial deficit and lack the ability to fund public goods and public services. On the contrary, if its authority of finance far exceeds its authority of office, there will be a problem with the government's efficiency in providing public goods and public services. Since financial revenues are basically from taxation, excessive authority of finance over the authority of office means that the residents in this region are paying excessive taxes without fully enjoying the public services covered by such taxes. In a state with several levels of government, the symmetry of the government's authority of finance and office is not "stiff" (that is, the tax revenues of a certain level of government must be equivalent to its expenditure), but "dynamic". When the authority of office of some local governments far exceeds their authority of finance, the government at the upper level will supplement the revenues of local governments with fiscal "subsidy" or "transfer payment". That is to say, a part of the expenditure of these governments is not from the tax revenues of their own level. Similarly, when the authority of finance of some local governments far exceeds their authority of office, the government at the upper level will require the local government of this level to submit a portion of their fiscal revenues. In other words, the revenue of the local government at this level will be "turned over" to cover some expenditure of the government of a higher level. In theory, such vertical fund flow in the form of "subsidy" or "turning over" is based on the allocation of the authority of office among governments of various levels. For instance, to build a trans-county or trans-city highway, the coordination of the construction by the provincial government is a choice incurring the minimum cost. But the fund used for building the highway should be raised by various relevant counties or cities *pro rata*. For another example, when it is going to construct a school, it can not only obtain the support of the county finance, but also the special subsidies from the central, provincial and municipal governments, as the graduates of this school may migrate nationwide. Therefore, the "symmetry" principle of the authority of finance and office determines that the allocation of the authority of finance is, to some extent, "directed" by the allocation of the authority of office.

The second principle is the "equalization" principle. Governments of higher levels will adjust the authority of office according to that of the finance. Besides, they have the right to balance the financial conditions of various regions on the basis of the difference of per capita financial expenditure level of each region so as to maintain the equalization of the financial expenditure levels of local governments. As far as a few public goods and public services are concerned, residents of each region have the right to enjoy a similar level or the lowest level of services. However, local governments with comparatively limited financial resources are unable to provide them residents with these services, so governments of higher levels will enhance the financial expenditure ability of these local governments by way of offering subsidies or transfer payment. The vertical financial redistribution is an significant content of financial system, too.

The third principle is the "efficiency" principle of financial expenditure. In addition to the two principles mentioned above, while preparing their respective financial systems, the government at the higher level and the government at the lower level may consider the problems of supervision and incentive. The so-called "supervision" means that the revenue and expenditure behaviors of the government at the lower level are regulated by a system so that it will not use fiscal funds with poor efficiency. In the supervision of the government at the lower level, besides the measures such as auditing and inspection, the government at the upper level may use "subsidy" or "transferred payment" in the financial system to influence the behaviors of the government at the lower level. Generally speaking, there are two kinds of financial subsidies. One is called "subsidy for general purpose", that is, no specific purpose is designated for such subsidy; the other is called "subsidy for earmarked or specific purpose", meaning that such subsidy has a specific purpose, and may not be used by the government at the lower level for any other purpose. In the two forms of subsidy, subsidy for general purpose does not have the function of supervision, as it is mainly used to meet the objective of "equalization" of financial expenditure, while subsidy for embarked or specific purpose has more influence on the government at the lower level. As the specific purpose of expenditure has been designated, the government at the upper level can justify its supervision of the use of the fund. The type, quantity and terms of payment of the fund for specific purpose will directly constrain the behaviors of the government at the lower level. The so-called "incentive" means the government at the upper level, in order to realize the sustainable and rapid growth of financial revenues, strives to encourage the local government to try its best to increase financial revenues by the financial system. For example, the government at the upper level may adopt a contractual system and leave all the incomes of the contracted work to the government at the lower level as incentive for financial revenue increase.

From the aforementioned three principles, it can be concluded that though we can measure and evaluate the relationship between the central government and local governments by the standards of efficiency and equity, each financial system framework has its unique characteristics as to what objectives it can realize or what objective is focused on at a certain historical period, in a certain social and political environment. Furthermore, the characteristics of the relationship between the central government and local governments are not determined by these principles but by the "wrestling" of the central government and local governments centering on these principles and objectives. The financial system between the central government and local governments, which seems to be the allocation of the authority of finance and office, is the allocation of power in reality. The administrative and personnel authority of the government is greatly determined by the financial authority. The negotiation over and struggle for financial authority between governments is more often than not one over and struggle for power by nature. Accordingly, the basic theoretical framework used to analyze the relationship between the central government and local governments may be summarized with the theory of "centralization" and "decentralization", which is also an essential theoretical concept for describing the relationship between the central government and local governments.

1.2 Centralization and Decentralization

In the relationship between the central government and local governments, "centralization" and "decentralization" of the authority of finance means that to what extent the central government can relegate the authority of office and of finance to local governments, or to what extent the local governments can autonomously use financial revenue and expenditure. A most typical example of the decentralization of the authority of finance is the enfeoffment system of the Spring and Autumn Period (700–476BC) and the Warring States Period (475–221BC) of China. In the contemporary world, the fiscal federalism of the United States is a typical representative, under which the government of each state has relatively independent financial autonomy. State governments have relatively independent authority to determine the tax types and tax rates, and to arrange and adjust public expenditure in their states. Diversified transfer payments between the central government and local governments and between states are standardized and fixed. The central government, which generally has its independent tax types and tax revenue sources, will not interfere the revenue and expenditure of local governments. For the centralization of the authority of finance, an extreme case is the "centralized revenue and centralized expenditure" financial system implemented in the early period (1949–1952) of New China. Under this system, local governments had no independent authority over finance. What's more, their financial revenues were entirely arranged by the central government. During this period, the authority of office, that is, the authority of expenditure, of local governments was also strictly controlled by the central government.

There is no decisive general rule to follow as to whether the financial system of a state should be centralized or decentralized. From the perspective of economic efficiency, decentralization of authority is more beneficial to the development of competition among local governments and to the improvement of the efficiency of public expenditure. However, from the perspective of fairness, excessive decentralization of authority tends to result in unbalanced economic growth among different regions, thus leading to the imbalance of the level of public expenditure among these regions. Such imbalance should be offset by the vertical transfer payment provided by the central government or the horizontal transfer payment among different regions. However, under the circumstances of excessive decentralization of authority, the central government is relatively weak in its capability of regulation, lacking the ability to mobilize the financial resources of local governments.

Unlike Western countries, China has been implementing a centralized political system in most of the time from the Qin Dynasty (221–207BC) to the present. The political system leads to a relatively high degree of centralization of financial power. Due to the lack of a system constraining the absolute power of the central government, excessive centralization tend to incur political instability just like excessive decentralization. Excessive local power tend to give rise to the disobedience of government orders, and may cause “feudal politics”, even local separatism and national splittism under extreme conditions. Excessive centralization of power in the central government tends to petrify the whole political and economic systems, making it difficult to have flexible and appropriate reaction to and settlement of problems in various places. As a result, minor local problems tend to spread and develop into serious nationwide problems, threatening political and national stability. The so-called “chaos brought into being by the decentralization of power and stagnation caused by the centralization of power” refers to such kind of situation.

The discussion about the centralization and decentralization of authority of finance is a hot issue in the field of political economics for the recent decade. Most countries in the world, be it a country with a federal financial system or with an unitary one, are dedicated to the reform of financial decentralization. Decentralization, so to speak, is a mainstream worldwide. It is generally believed that decentralization may grant local governments more autonomy, thus enhancing the operation efficiency of the entire economic and political systems, and that the competition mechanism caused by decentralization may also bring about more equal allocation of resources. Meanwhile, however, some scholars have discovered different (or contradictory) evidences. For instance, Davoodi and Zou think that there is no significant connection between decentralization and economic growth, while De Mello has found that decentralization may lead to more unbalanced allocation of financial resources among different regions. Some scholars have pointed out that decentralization is conditional and it comes with a price. Given that some necessary prerequisites are unavailable, decentralization of the authority of finance will not only fail to improve efficiency but also produce some unexpected consequences. These prerequisites are all related to the modes of government behaviors. Therefore, the most important factor is not decentralization or centralization but in government behaviors. For decentralization and centralization, government behaviors are exogenous rather than endogenous, which serve as the prerequisite for, instead of an outcome of, our understanding of the decentralization framework.

Among the above-mentioned prerequisites, the most important are incompleteness in the accountability system for officials and the consequent soft budget problem. Soft budget constraint is a widely used concept. In terms of finance, the soft budget constraint mainly refers to a situation under which the expenditure of a government at a lower level exceeds the budget. However, this government is not responsible for filling the fiscal gap. Usually, the gap will be filled by bailout or borrowings of the government at a higher level afterwards. With respect to borrowing, the government at a lower level believes that they have no or only a partial responsibility to pay their debts. Thus the financial burden will be borne by the government at a higher level eventually. The existence of a soft budget constraint will encourage excessive expenditure or unreasonable spending budget by the government at a lower level, which may eventually lead to inefficiency. Low efficiency arising from excessive centralization is certainly relevant with the soft budget constraint (see the classic analysis of Kornai). Furthermore, if something is seriously wrong with the soft budget constraint, the decentralization of authority result in an increase in the incidence of corruption instead of efficiency. Under this circumstance, inequality in resource distribution will be exacerbated, making the goal of equalizing resource distribution proposed by some researchers in this field impossible to achieve. That is to say, unlike the economic sphere, the field of politics will not be made more effective by relieving the soft budget constraint by means of privatization and decentralization. Although decentralization may intensify the competitions among local governments, such competitions will not necessarily eliminate the soft budget constraint. These competitions may take the form of investment promotion and capital introduction, or a mushrooming of "image projects", for efficiency has never been considered as a leading indicator of the performance of local governments. Thus, a general discussion on the advantages and disadvantages of decentralization and centralization is far from being enough to help us understand the relationship between the central government and local governments, the East and the Midwest China, as well as the government and enterprises. A real thorough analysis should cover empirical researches of government behaviors.

In terms of government behaviors in China since the reform and opening up, many scholars, who noticed that the fiscal relationship between the central government and local governments has an impact on the behaviors of local governments as well as China's economic growth, have conducted many empirical studies in this aspect.

The theory of fiscal decentralization, a basic start for the study of this field, holds that at the premise that local resources and production factors can flow freely and residents can "vote with their feet", fiscal decentralization of local governments decided by the central government may bring about a benign regional competition among the formers and thus effectively enhance economic growth. Noticing the positive role of local governments in local industrialization quite early, a few scholars represented by Jean C.Oi use the term "local state corporatism" to explain the rise of township enterprises and other local industries. She argues that under the fiscal responsibility system established in the mid-1980s, local governments can obtain not only a fiscal revenue higher than the base quota of the contract, but also an extra-budget revenue in the form of profits turned in by township enterprises, which gives them a great impetus to encourage the establishment of township enterprises.

Many scholars found that since the mid-1980s, the fiscal responsibility system has been essentially a decentralization system chosen by the central government for local governments. This system, whose the basic mechanism is the regional competition based on fiscal decentralization, has remarkably promoted local economic growth in China. In addition, rapid growth of entire local economy proves that the fiscal responsibility system can benefit the development of local economy. According to the province-by-province quantitative study by Lin Justin Yifu and

Liu Zhiqiang, this system has played a significant role in promoting the increase of local GDP. The research and Qian Yingyi and several other scholars shows that this promotive effect is achieved through regional competitions among local governments. Some scholars further discovered that if the degree of decentralization were measured by fiscal expenditure, China's economic growth ever since the reform and opening up could be perfectly explained with the theory of fiscal decentralization no matter under the fiscal responsibility system or the tax-sharing system.

However, an important issue has not been addressed by these studies yet, namely the earth-shaking changes in the relationship between the central government and local governments ever since the implementation of the tax-sharing system. Most obviously, from the perspective of income, the tax-sharing reform of 1994 aimed at centralization rather than decentralization. Although the expenditure pattern of the central government has not witnessed obvious changes if measured by the expenditure method, the distribution of income has undoubtedly brought about great changes in the behaviors of the central government as well as local governments, leading to the pattern of local competition as well as behaviors of local governments. How should we understand the relationship between such changes and current social and economic development in China?

This book examines the behavior pattern of local governments based on an analysis of the dramatic changes in the relationship between the central government and local governments ever since the reform and opening up and our understanding of the current economic and social development mode as well as the incentive mechanism. We find that the relationship between the central government and local governments has witnessed two significant changes since the founding of the People's Republic of China. The first change is the implementation of the fiscal responsibility system in the 1980s. The second one is the implementation of the tax-sharing system in the mid-1950s. The former has thoroughly changed the basic framework of fiscal centralization and thus ushered in the transition from fiscal centralization to decentralization, establishing an economic-social development pattern dominated by local competitions and characterized by local governments' encouragement of the establishment of enterprises and enlargement of the scale of enterprises for the sake of promoting the development of local industrialization. The latter centralized fiscal authority, but retained a decentralized governance, leaving the dominant pattern of local competitions unchanged. However, the fiscal centralization has ushered in a shift of local governments' focus from enterprise-running to land-managing and city-managing in the pursuit for revenue, which objectively realized the rapid development of urbanization and determined the basic pattern and characteristics of this process in China, namely a "trinity" of land, finance and bank investments.

The key to understanding this urbanization pattern lies in the knowledge about land expropriation, development and transfer system. Therefore, we attempt to explore the interactions between the central government and local governments in the making and implementation of land policies. The intertwined land and fiscal power divisions constitute a basic and important clue for our understanding of the current social and economic development in China. Before we set out to analyze the history and mechanism, a review of the historical background before the reform and opening up in China is necessary for the clarification of the historical situation under which fiscal decentralization evolved.

1.3 "Retaking" and "Delegating" Authority

China started an overall construction of the socialist economic and political system in 1949. A new framework for the relationship between the central government and local governments was built on the basis of the construction. Although the traditional five-level administrative relationship was inherited by this framework, a highly-centralized authority took shape rapidly along with the establishment and development of the socialist planned economy system.

A highly centralized control was exerted by the central government over revenues and expenditures soon after the founding of the People's Republic of China in order to stabilize prices, solve financial difficulties, and support the war to resist U.S. aggression and aid Korea. In this system, the collection, spending and scheduling of all agricultural taxes paid in grain, except for a local surcharge of 10–15%, were under the control of the central government. In terms of taxes, the scheduling, allocation and use of all tariffs, salt/commodity taxes, industrial and commercial taxes, etc. were also under the control of the central government, except for a few approved local taxes. Fiscal expenditure, which mainly covered military and administrative expenditures and investment, was also subject to the unified registration and supply standard determined by the central government.

This highly centralized system was adjusted during the first five-year plan (1953–1957). In 1953, China started the socialist reform on agriculture, handicraft industry and capitalist industry and commerce. Originally scheduled to be finished in over ten years, the reform was accomplished in five years.

In 1953, the aforementioned unified control of fiscal revenue and expenditure by the central government was replaced by a distribution of fiscal revenues and expenditures between the central government and local governments, including provincial (municipal) and county (municipal) governments. The sharing of revenue by category between the central government and local governments under the unified leadership of the former was introduced in 1954, dividing fiscal revenues into three categories, namely fixed revenue, revenue for sharing at constant ratio and revenue regulated by the central government. Local budgets were subjected to the annual ratification of the central government. In case that fixed revenue exceeds the normal expenditure of local governments, the remainder would no longer be turned over to the central government, but divided with it according to the ratio of the remainder in fixed revenues, which was the calculation basis of revenue for sharing at constant ratio. Such fixed ratio were re-calculated every year. Should local budgets exceed local revenues, local fixed revenue and the fixed-ratio part would be used to make up the balance. The insufficient part (if any) would be paid with the regulated revenue by the central government.

It seemed that the local finance was independent to some degree under this fiscal system. However, due to the fact that the fixed revenue allocated to local governments accounted for only a minor potion of the total fiscal revenue and the sharing proportion were subject to year-by-year re-calculation according to the difference between income and expenditure of the previous year, the proportion of the next-year turn over to the central government would increase sharply along with its rapid growth in income. Therefore, this system only meant a preliminary fiscal division between the central government and local governments, leaving the situation characterized by high fiscal centralization unchanged. From the perspective of the collection scope of fiscal revenue, the central government and local governments accounted for 45 and 55% respectively during the first five years, while the actual proportions based on the fiscal system were 80 versus 20% in terms of fiscal revenue and 75 versus 25% in terms of fiscal expenditure, which was undoubtedly an embodiment of centralization. By the completion of the first five-year plan and the socialist transformation, the basic framework for economic and fiscal relationship between the central government and local governments in China had been set up. The relationship was mainly characterized by the direct top-down control over governance and allocation of most of the nationwide human/financial/material resources by the central government. The control was achieved via various governing systems established in all industrial and economic sectors in the form of planned quotas. Specifically, almost all important enterprises were included in the top-down system for direct governance Others were subject to indirect regional governance, but the allocation of their revenues and profits was still controlled by the central government.

The highly-centralized governing system during the first five-year plan was unable to arouse the enthusiasm of local governments as the powers mostly remained with the central government. As early as 1956, the central government realized that problems caused by high centralization. In "On Ten Relationships", Mao Zedong noted that China should strengthen the authority of local governments, so that they might serve in an enlarged stretch of affairs more independently. From 1956 to 1957, the central government issued a series of documents, helping the decentralization progress in a planned manner by delegating the authority in enterprises/commercial/fiscal administration to local governments.

The central government initiated an overall devolution of authority in early 1958, which was the first large-scale reform of this kind since the founding of the PRC. In terms of administration, the originally weakened greater administrative areas were valued again, and seven collaboration areas, namely, Northeast China, North China, East China, South China, Central China, Northwest China, and Southwest China, were determined, all of which were required to establish regional economy under a complete industrial system comprising large backbone enterprises and economic centers. Before long, subordinate provinces of the greater administrative areas were also required to explore the ways of establishing independent industrial systems. With regard to enterprise management, as the large-scale devolution of governance over enterprises administered by the central government to local governments evolved, over 1200 enterprises remained directly under the central government by 1958, accounting for only 12% of the total number, namely more than 9300, of 1957. Meanwhile, the proportion of industrial output value of such enterprises to the total industrial output value also decreased to 13.8%. In the meanwhile, the autonomy and control of enterprises had been intensified rapidly, with mandatory indexes related to enterprise administration reduced from 12 to 4. The enterprises' authority over personnel and financial affairs was also strengthened significantly. As a result of the reform of the fiscal system, local fiscal revenue only need to be subject to re-calculation every five years, instead of every year. Meantime, the revenue base as well as spending authority had also witnessed rapid enhancement. Along with these practices, the central government modified the planned quotas drastically.

In *Sixty Working Methods* (*draft*) forwarded by the Central Committee of the Communist Party of China in February, 1958, Mao Zedong proposed to separate production and planning and, as a supplement, establish a system of planning characterized by a combination of top-down governance and regional administration, with a highlight on the later. All the province/municipality/autonomous regions were required to adjust their industrial and agricultural production index and endowed with the autonomy in local construction investments, human/financial/material resources and public utility projects. Against this backdrop, only one index, i.e., the index of products and production, remained in the industrial production plan for the second five-year, screening out the other five indexes included in the first five-year plan. The infrastructure program only supervised the investment and major constructions of the year. Meanwhile, the range of industrial products under the unified administration of the State Development Planning Commission (SDPC) was sharply narrowed. The proportion of fiscal revenue directly paid to the central government to the total decreased to 20% in 1959. The authority in other production-related aspects, such as infrastructure investment approval, material distribution and recruitment planning, were also delegated to lower levels. Thus local governments basically enjoyed autonomy in infrastructure investment. Only 429 types of materials were still under the unified distribution and administration of the central government in 1958, compared with 532 in 1957. In 1959 the number further decreased to 285. In addition, the number of staff and urban residents had also increased dramatically.

Despite its spur to economic growth, the overall devolution had caused serious problems, which mainly included the shocking proneness to boasting and exaggeration and severe imbalance in economic structure rooted in false index pursuit of local governments in the process of overall devolution. From 1958 to 1960, the local governments at all levels were boasting about their false achievements in steel and grain output, resulting in the appearance of totally falsified data about the output of major products administered by the central government. There was a nationwide ardor for establishing independent economic systems and various industrial projects, among which the number of large and medium-sized projects even exceeded the total during the first five year, unveiling a severely deformed economic structure. During this period, the heavy and light industries witnessed a growth rate of 2.33 and 47% respectively, while agricultural output decreased by

22.7%. As a result, it engendered substantial decrease in national income and fiscal revenue, resulting in a wide-spreading disaster in agriculture.

The famine was followed by a period of economic contraction and the adjustment that were mainly characterized by the central government's re-taking of authority in national economic planning and administration devolved to local governments during the "Great Leap Forward". A re-centralization in administration and economic management was carried out from 1961 to 1966. Regarding finance, the sharing-in-total fiscal system was implemented so that local fiscal powers and resources could be taken back by the central government. Under such a system, the division of fixed revenues between the central government and local governments was erased. What's more, the total budget revenue of the central government and local governments should be first calculated. Each province should subtract its budget expenditures from the respective calculated budget revenue, thus the sharing between the central government and local governments was determined according to the proportion of the balance to budget revenue. Different from sharing in revenue by category, the proportion under this system was subject to yearly re-calculation based on the balance between revenue and expenditures of the previous year, which means in case of excessive growth in the revenue of a local government, the part supposed to be turned over to the central government would increase sharply, quite similar to the situation during the first five-year period. The centralization of economic administration authority helped end the economic chaos caused by the "Great Leap Forward", playing a significant role in the recovery of national economy.

Following the start of the "Cultural Revolution", the central government proposed a basic idea about national economy giving priority to regional administration, which required that central institutions to be downsized and merged. Thus, 90 ministries and commissions directly under the State Council were reduced to 27, and only 18% of the manning was retained by 1970. Meanwhile, the administration authority of a large number of enterprises directly under central ministries and commissions were also transferred to local governments. There remained over 1600 industrial enterprises directly under central ministries and commissions in 1970, whose output accounting for only 6% of the gross industrial output, while in 1965, there were 10,533 industrial enterprises whose output accounting for 42.2% of the gross industrial output. Regarding infrastructure, local governments were given enhanced authority over investment management and required to shoulder all-round responsibilities for construction projects in line with national regulations. By 1974, the investments were distributed according to the ratio of 4:3:3, i.e., the central government and local governments were entitled to 40% and 30% of the total investment respectively, with the remaining 30% subject to joint management. As for materials administration, the 579 kinds of materials subject to unified allocation presided over by the central government or administered by respective ministries in 1966 were reduced to 217 by 1972. The administration over distribution and supply of materials of enterprises was devolved to local governments. This was the second large-scale devolution following the "Great Leap Forward".

The devolution starting from the mid-late 1960s considerably expanded the scale of investment in fixed assets, initiating another index and development rate-based campaign of local governments. The layer-on-layer (from the central government to local governments) inflation announced another high index-based contest among local governments, bringing about a series of problems including an imbalanced national economy. The rapid investment expansion confronted undersupply of raw materials, equipments and power, resulting in unsatisfied indexes, a decline in the quality of industrial products, serious equipment damages, lower labor productivity, etc.

During this period, though complicated, the fiscal relationship between the central government and local governments was on the whole in line with the logic of "authority-re-taking—authority devolving" in economic administration. During the large-scale devolution lasting from 1971 to 1973, the fiscal responsibility system was implemented by the central government and local governments. The content of the system included ratified revenues and expenditures, contracted revenues and expenditures and a guaranteed turnover (or subsidy for deficit) to the central government. "Ratified revenues and expenditures" refers to determining the respective revenue/expenditure scopes (viz. the limits of validity of fiscal and administrative authority) of the central government and local governments. "Contracted revenues and expenditures" mean that provinces with more revenues than expenditures should turn the surplus over to the central government, while deficit-ridden provinces would be provided with a deficit-based subsidy by the central government. Once determined, the contracted amount would not be modified, hence the local governments could keep the surplus if they had more revenues and less expenditures. The central government would not provide any subsidy even if a fiscal deficit appeared in these regions.

Compared with the aforementioned two systems, this is a relatively thorough quota-based responsibility system encouraging local governments to enhance their respective revenues, but it made the revenue centralization of the central government difficult. Therefore, this system had been implemented for only one year, i.e., during the year of 1971. According to the modifications made by the central government in 1972, if it was less than CNY 100 million, the surplus would be retained completely by the local government. The extra portion (if any) should be turned over to the central government. This system was unapplicable to municipalities or counties.

From 1974 to 1975, the fiscal system of China was characterized by a fixed sharing ratio for the portion no higher than baseline and an unfixed sharing ratio for the portion higher than baseline. A combination of sharing-by-category and sharing-in-total was adopted. Since then, China confronted great fiscal difficulties, for the desired rapid growth in fiscal revenue had not been achieved by devolution. As a result, the sharing-in-total fiscal system first implemented during the centralization period (1959–1970) was restored.

In short, the fiscal system of China underwent "the re-taking of authority" three times and "devolution of authority" twice (which took place during the "Great Leap Forward" and the "Cultural Revolution" respectively) from 1949 to the reform and opening up. Compared with the re-taking of authority, devolution has a most distinctly characterized by its encouragement of a substantial rise of investment in local fixed assets. Against a broader social background, devolution was also related to the index-oriented competition among local governments. There were both similarities and differences between the fiscal "devolution" and the increase in fiscal authority of local governments rising from the fiscal responsibility system implemented after the reform and opening up.

First, this devolution campaign was launched on the absolute premise that economic resources should be under the overall control of the State. Under the socialist planned system, there was no market or commodity economy, so almost all of the social/economic resources were under the control of the government. Therefore, the practices of re-taking and devolution of authority must be understood as the incentive for and adjustment of the economic structure as well a regulation of the development speed by the State through administrative means. This basic mode of this attempt was to devolve authority when the economy was suffering from stagnation and to re-talke authority when the development of economy is too speedy and chaotic. Under such a planned system, a stagnation arising from the re-taking of authority and the chaos caused by the devolution of authority were typical for the relationship between the local government and local governments during this period.

Second, fiscal devolution cannot be implemented separately under the planned economic system. It should be accompanied by devolution of authority in investment and enterprise management to local governments. Certainly, in view of the characteristics of the planned economy, the authority of administering agriculture, commerce, even the authority finance and office would usually be delegated to local governments along with the aforesaid decentralization of authority in investment and enterprise management. During this process of decentralization, the output of major products vital to national economy and people's livelihood was a key indicator in evaluating the performance of local governments. Delegating capital authority to lower levels was a basic condition indispensable for the organization of competitions and the achievement of goals.

Thirdly, both the re-taking and devolution of authority were implemented under the high centralization in other aspects of the central government. Higher devolution in one aspect has usually made the centralization in other aspects more severe. Authority should be retaken or delegated under a careful control over manning or ideological/political/military affairs. This kind of devolution made it difficult for local governments to form an independent consciousness of an interest subject. Furthermore, all competitions were based on the index control of the central government, which differed in nature from those of local governments brought into being by the decentralization implemented after the reform and opening up.

Chapter 2
Fiscal Responsibility System

The 30 years following the reform and opening may be divided into two periods (15 years for each) marked by the adoption of the tax-sharing system. During the first 15 years, the success in rural reform and prosperity of township enterprises were coupled with the first upsurge of industrialization following the reform and opening up, which was basically driven by the responsibility system. This has been a significant reform on the rural production management system starting from practices of the joint contract responsibility system in rural areas. The contract system is characterized by a separation between ownership and use rights, whereby the use rights and usufruct are transferred to users on the premise that the ownership shall remain unchanged in nature. This has been a strategy typical for gradual reform, which not only maintains the public or collective ownership, but also arouses the enthusiasm of individuals effectively. From early 1980s to the mid-1990s, the responsibility system played a key role in China's reform. Any reform-related problem confronted by the country throughout the 1980s was solved neatly. First implemented in rural areas, it was gradually adopted by enterprises, and introduced to facilitate the interaction between the central government and local governments.

2.1 Connotation and Evolution of the Fiscal Responsibility System

The fiscal responsibility system was put into trial use in 1980. After several trials, it was implemented across the country in 1988. According to the basic principle of this system, the central government contracts out local fiscal revenues and expenditures to provincial financial units, entitling local governments to a pre-determined percentage of the surplus revenue. However, the central government will reduce the subsidy for unbalanced revenues and expenditures caused by a decline in revenues,

F. Zhou and M. Tan, *Relationship between the Central Government and Local Governments of Contemporary China*, Social Development Experiences in China,
DOI 10.1007/978-981-10-4388-8_2

or even offer no subsidy at all. This was basically consistent with the principle of fixing farm output quotas for each household and the fiscal responsibility system applied to enterprises.

In the previous chapter, it is noted that devolution was realized by gradually delegating the authority over distributing materials vital to national economy and over enterprises management. The central government achieved the regulation of national economic operations by means of subtly devoluting and re-taking powers. Under this system, the regional administration system dominated by local governments was often fragmented by the direct vertical administration by the central government, leaving the local governments neither complete authority over economic administration nor interests independent from the central government. This was obviously manifested by the fiscal system between the central government and local governments. Although adjusted correspondingly during the devolution process, neither sharing-in-revenue by category nor the fixed sharing system provided stable stimulus to local governments, for under the planned economic regulation system, modifications were frequently made to the fiscal system as the authority over materials distribution and enterprises management shifted back and forth between vertical control and regional administration, despite of the considerations given to this issue by the central government. The central government usually did not fulfill its promise to local governments during policy making, and it has also been difficult for local governments to negotiate with the central government. Therefore, the fiscal system provided extremely limited incentives to local government to enhance their respective revenues. In this sense, these practices shall be referred to as devolution of powers, rather than decentralization.

The fiscal responsibility system has been a step forward decentralization. The general idea in this system is "responsibility", which stood on the premise of a clear separation of authority over revenues and expenditures between the central government and local governments. The responsibility delegated to local governments was based on the total revenues and expenditures, rejecting any intervention in the entitlement of local governments to gains from revenues growth and in expenditures reduction. This responsibility "package" actually vested local governments with relatively stable authorities over supplies distribution and enterprises management, and thus gradually helped local governments to gain subject consciousness, preventing the regional administration system from being fragmented by vertical governance.

The fiscal responsibility system can only be truly implemented on the premise that the State should no longer rely on the vertical and regional administration systems for regulating economic operations. Therefore, although it is the correct approach to dealing with the relationship between the central government and local governments explicitly chosen as early as the beginning of the 1980s, the fiscal responsibility system actually experienced a tortuous process in gradual improvement and stabilization, as the national economic administration system remained unchanged and the vertical and regional administrations still played a role. From 1980 to 1984, the fiscal system was constantly adjusted by the central government. For example, as a result of the decline of revenues turnover to the central government, the promise of principally maintaining the fiscal system with a designated scope of revenues/expenditures and responsibility contracts at various levels for 5 successive years made in 1980 was actually broken in 1981, compelling many local governments to retake the sharing-in-total and proportion-based responsibility contract approach. In order to truly give full play to the contract system in the decentralization process, the planned economic system needs to be transformed into a market economic system.

The period from 1980 to 1993 can be divided into three stages according to the evolution of the responsibility system.

2.1.1 *Pilot Stage (1980–1984)*

As early as in 1977, the central government piloted the fixed-ratio based sharing system in Jiangsu Province, where the percentage of turnover was determined as per the proportion of total final expenditures to total revenues in 1976 (the turnover and retention percentages were 52 and 48% in 1977, respectively.), and should remain unchanged for 4 successive years in revenues sharing. This was actually what the fixed revenue sharing-in-total system would imply. During these four years, from every 1 yuan in the revenues pool, the central government and the provincial government of Jiangsu took 0.58 and 0.42 yuan, respectively. The retention should be subject to the decision of the provincial government. Theoretically, as long as the proportion is fixed, the absolute retainable amount would increase along with the growth of fiscal revenues. However, as some expenditure items of the central government were included under the expenditure responsibility of Jiangsu Province, they were partially returned to the central government in order to relieve the burden of the provincial government, and correspondingly, the retention percentage was lowered. Since 1978, the turnover and retention percentages were changed to 61 and 39%, respectively.

Since 1980, the central government implemented a fiscal system characterized by designated scope of revenues and expenditures and multi-level responsibility contracts in 15 provinces. Compared with the revenue sharing-in-total system, this was based on a fixed sharing ratio, similar to the sharing-by-category system implemented from 1953 to 1958. The key to this system was to draw a responsibility base according to the respective scope of fiscal revenues and expenditures of the central government and the provincial government, and correspondingly determine the turnover and retention percentages, which should remain unchanged for five successive years. However, faced with a fall in fiscal revenues, the central government embarked on modifying this system in 1981. By the end of June 1982, of the 15 provinces, 10 recovered the sharing-in-total system; and by 1983, it was horse and foot, making the multi-level responsibility system a shadow, except that the all-round responsibility system was adopted by Guangdong and Fujian (deficit-ridden as it was), to which the key was a shift from proportional turnover and proportional subsidy to quota turnover and quota subsidy, respectively.

According to quota turnover and quota subsidy, local governments should be entitled to 100% of the portion in excess of the said base amount. These may be considered pilots of the quota-based system launched by the central government, and this fiscal system has been maintained in Guangdong and Fujian ever since.

2.1.2 *Transition Stage (1985–1987)*

At this stage, the responsibility system implemented by the central government and local governments was characterized by separate categories of taxes, designated scope of revenues and expenditures and multi-level responsibility contracts. During this period, although 17 provincial units still shared the revenues in total with the central government, a significant change occurred to the system, as the sharing ratio should be maintained for five successive years, rather than only one year. This was a great stimulus for local governments to enhance their respective revenues. Just like Guangdong, Heilongjiang also adopted the quota turnover-based all-round responsibility system, whereby the limit of turnover from surplus was CNY 6.5 billion. In addition, following the practices of Fujian, Jilin, Jiangxi, Shaanxi, Gansu, Hubei, and Sichuan adopted quota subsidy. So, the number of provincial governments embracing the quota-based contract system increased from two at the first stage to seven. Other minorities and frontier provinces implemented the budget management system, which was actually equal to the quota subsidy system.

2.1.3 *Comprehensive Implementation Stage (1988–1993)*

At this stage, the fiscal system of dividing revenues and expenditures between the central government and local governments and holding each responsible for balancing their respective budgets was relatively thoroughly implemented. Altogether 39 provincial units (provinces, autonomous regions, or municipalities directly under the central government or under separate state planning) adopted six different approaches to the responsibility system.

1. Designated revenues increase rate-based contract: The key to this approach was to determine the year-on-year revenues increasing rate and the retention/turnover percentages. Where the revenues growth rate exceeded the designated year-on-year increasing rate, local governments should be entitled to the premium portion and retentions by a pre-determined percentage within the designated rate, the remainder should be turned over to the central government. For example, for Beijing, the designated increasing rate and the retention percentage were 4 and 50%, respectively. So, if the revenues growth rate of Beijing exceeded 4%, 104% of the revenues of the previous year should be subject to a 50–50 sharing with the central government. Assume that the revenues in 1987

and 1988 were CNY 10 billion and 11 billion, respectively. According to the designated increasing rate, there was a premium of CNY 0.6 billion, which should be retained by the municipal government of Beijing; and the remaining CNY 10.4 billion should be 50–50 shared between the central and municipal governments. Therefore, the final turnover to the central government and retentions by the municipal government of Beijing should be CNY 5.2 and 5.8 billion, respectively. The following provincial units adopted this approach (each followed by their designated increasing rate and retention percentage, respectively): Beijing (4, 50%), Hebei (4.5, 70%), Liaoning (3.5, 58.25%), Shenyang (4, 30.29%), Haerbin (5, 45%), Jiangsu (5, 41%), Zhejiang (6.5, 61.47%), Ningbo (5.3, 27.93%), Henan (5, 80%), and Chongqing (4, 33.5%).

2. Sharing in total: This is basically the same with the previously-adopted revenue sharing-in-total system. Three provincial units embraced this approach, namely Tianjin (45.5%), Shanxi (87.55%) and Anhui (77.5%).
3. Sharing in total plus sharing in increase: According to this approach, the revenues may be divided into two parts, namely the portion within the base amount that should be subject to sharing in total and the portion in excess that should be subject to sharing in increase. Three provincial units adopted this approach (each followed by the percentage of sharing in total and the percentage of sharing in increase, respectively): Dalian (37.74, 27.76%), Qingdao (16, 34%) and Wuhan (17, 25%).
4. Designated turnover increase-based contract: In this approach, factors other than the year-on-year turnover increase would not be considered. Only two provinces adopted this approach (followed by their respective turnover amounts and designated increase rates): Guangdong (CNY 1.413 billion, 9%) and Hunan (CNY 0.8 billion, 7%).
5. Quota turnover: According to this approach, in case of any surplus (an excess of revenues over expenditures), the turnover amount should be fixed, rather than based on the year-on-year increase amount. Three provincial units adopted this approach (followed by their respective quotas): Shanghai (CNY 10.5 billion), Shandong (CNY 0.3 billion) and Heilongjiang (CNY 2.9 billion).
6. Quota subsidy: According to this approach, in case of deficit, the subsidy amount should be fixed, rather than based on the year-on-year decrease amount. 16 provincial units adopted this approach.

Complicated as it may be, the responsibility system can be basically divided into the following four categories:

1. Sharing in total, whereby the sharing percentages should be subject to yearly recalculation;
2. Fixed ratio-based sharing, whereby the sharing percentages usually remain constant for several successive years;
3. Proportional turnover or subsidy whereby, based on the responsibility system, any surplus should be subject to ratio-based turnover, or any deficit may be

relieved by a subsidy. The said ratio might be either fixed or include a year-on-year increase rate; and
4. Quota turnover or subsidy, commonly known as the all-round responsibility system, whereby the surplus may be wholly retained by local governments as long as their revenues exceed the quota.

Approaches (1–4) have presented a continuous spectrum of enhancement in encouraging local governments to increase their respective revenues. As the first embracer of the quota turnover-based all-round responsibility system, Guangdong Province was the fastest in economic development and thus the highest in fiscal revenues, standing as a perfect model for other provinces. the responsibility system has related local economic development to fiscal revenues of the local government. Therefore, local governments had to accelerate local economic development in order to enhance their respective fiscal revenues. As the all-round responsibility system was adopted by more and more provinces, regional economic development competition became increasingly intense. Under the responsibility system, for the revenues of local governments were directly linked to economic development, such competition achieved not only political purposes but also economic benefits, and as a result of fiscal decentralization, provided sustainable stimulus to local governments.

Local governments below the provincial level also adopted the same approach as that implemented between the central government and provincial governments, namely the responsibility system. Here we take the relationship between governments at the county level and governments at the township level as an example for explanation. Index or task-based package responsibility is the most typical of the responsibility system, based on which, governments at the township level would be either rewarded (in case of surplus) or punished (in case of deficit) according to their balance of revenues and expenditures. This system should be subject to adjustment every 3–5 years, which has mainly focused on the surplus reward/deficit punishment measures and expenditure liability, as the case may be. The following is a discussion of this system from perspectives of task allocation, surplus and deficit.

Under the responsibility system, a "target" is usually referred to as a "base", and surplus and deficit are held relative to the "base". The bases for different governments at the township level within the same county might be different. As the major component was tax revenues under budget control, it has been known as "revenues base". It should be determined as per normal tax. In adjusting the fiscal system (if necessary), the revenues base should be determined based on the average revenues of the previous cycle or the previous three years, floating as per the tax base during the corresponding cycle. For example, should an enterprise be introduced into or established in a township in a definite cycle, the increase in tax would be considered in the determination of a new base for the following cycle which, once determined, should remain unchanged. For example, if determined as CNY 1 million, the base should remain constant for the coming 3–5 years. However, a great number of counties were found in much more complicated situations, and for some relatively developed townships, the county government would usually assign a target in addition to the base. Although the base remained unchanged within the corresponding cycle, the target amount would increase by a certain percentage. Therefore, this would be a double-responsibility system combining a fixed base and a year-on-year increasing target amount.

Should the actual revenues exceed the base, the township would obtain a beyond-base surplus; should it also exceed the target amount, there would also be a beyond-target amount surplus; should it exceed the base but fall short of the target amount, the township would obtain a beyond-base surplus but no beyond-target amount surplus; and should it even fail to reach the base, there would be a deficit. In order to encourage townships to enhance their respective revenues, reward and punishment measures were usually included in the county/township fiscal system, including:

Sharing in surplus: Any beyond-base/target amount surplus would be shared by the governments at the two levels as per a pre-determined proportion. In most cases, the portion retained by the government at the township level exceeded that turned over to the county government. It is also found that the percentages of sharing in beyond-base surplus were different from those in beyond-target amount surplus.

Retaining total surplus: In this approach, the township may retain the beyond-base surplus and the beyond-target amount surplus wholly. In some cases, only the beyond-target amount surplus could be retained wholly, while the beyond-base surplus should be shared with the county government.

For any township maintaining surplus in successive years, its total revenues (or actual revenues) would consist of three portions: base + beyond-base revenues + beyond-target amount revenues. According to the surplus distribution approaches, the fiscal responsibility system implemented between governments at the county and township levels might be preliminarily divided into two categories, namely sharing in surplus and retaining total surplus. Thus, how was the base distributed between governments at the county and township levels? And how did those deficit-ridden townships fill the gap?

This will be illustrated by introducing the expenditure liability of the government at the township level. Any surplus would be shared by the township as a fiscal reward granted by the county government and thus may be used freely. The portion within the base should be shared with the county government based on the expenditure base, determined as per the daily expenditures of the township. Generally speaking, the fiscal expenditure liability can be understood as insurance for salary, operation and construction. Salary insurance guarantees the payment of due salaries to the staff of administration and business sectors; operation insurance covers the daily office expenses of administration and business sectors, including costs of office supplies/conference, travel/entertainment expenses, etc., usually determined as per the size of manning within the fiscal scope; construction insurance includes the routine public maintenance and construction projects. In most of the townships in Midwest China, only two of the three items of insurance have been basically fulfilled, namely salary and operation insurances. In fact, in most regions, the base was determined mainly as per total salary and daily operation costs; and in financial difficulty-ridden counties and townships, the operation insurance was even hardly fulfilled, and daily expenses were also excluded from the expenditure base.

In case of any surplus, the revenues base would be usually higher than the expenditure base. Under the fiscal system of most counties/townships, such difference would be included in the revenues of the county government and thus subject to turnover which, together with the part from sharing in surplus, has been referred to as "turnover within the system". In such a way, the actual revenues of a surplus township may be divided into two parts under the above-mentioned system, namely turnover within the system comprising the excess of the revenues base over the expenditure base and revenues retention comprising the expenditure base and the retentions from sharing in surplus.

Deficit-ridden governments at the township level would be faced with more complicated situations. As the expenditure base would be higher than the revenues base, a subsidy should be granted to such governments in order to guarantee due payments of salaries and operational expenses, referred to as "subsidy within the system". The amount of such subsidy should be equal to the difference between the expenditure base and the revenues base. In case of any surplus in a certain year, the excess of revenues over the base should be subject to sharing-in-surplus or retaining-total-surplus, and the subsidy within the system would be fully granted; in case of deficit, the subsidy within the system would be also fully granted, but the gap would not be covered by the county government as a punishment for the deficit. So the actual amount received by a township government would be equal to the sum of its actual revenues and subsidy within the system, and the total amount would hardly catch up the expenditure base, for the gap would not be covered by the county government and remain for its own makeup.

From the above analysis, we can see that the fiscal responsibility system implemented between governments at the county and township levels included various modalities. All these modalities provided a great stimulus to the governments at the township level. A surplus-achieving township could be entitled to all the excess of actual revenues over the base; and for a deficit-ridden township, it has been unnecessary to satisfy the expenditure base as long as it reached the revenues base. This system helped us a lot to understand the behaviors of the governments at the grassroots level.

Theoretically, this system provided a stimulus similar to that in enterprises management. As the core of the micro operating mechanism of "corporatism of local governments" proposed by Jean C. Oi, this was one of the primary impetuses behind the corporatization of local governments. In local practices, the governments at the township level were not blindly aimed at revenues maximization in their pursuit of maximum disposable revenues. Under the fiscal responsibility system, a rapid increase in the revenues of a certain cycle would enhance the revenues base and the target amount of the following cycle, leading to magnified difficulties in satisfying the target of the following cycle as well as reduced revenues. Therefore, the behavior strategy of governments at the township level should be understood in the context of the tenure system for officials thereof. An official might try his/her best to increase the fiscal revenues during his/her tenure in order to achieve rapid promotion; however, should it be expected that he/she would hold the office for quite a long time, he/she might exert moderate control over the revenues growth rate. For governments at the county level, such periodic adjustments made to the base and the target amount would not only intensify the incentives for governments at the township level to enhance their respective revenues, but also guarantee the fiscal revenues at the county level would not decrease significantly and even achieve rapid growth in the following period. In addition, by adjusting the proportion of sharing in surplus, the county government provided incentives to those townships that had witnessed a too high or too low growth rate of revenues. For example, an enhanced proportion of the retainable would encourage the governments at the township level to increase their revenues; however, by lowering this proportion, the revenues obtained by these governments may be centralized or used for planning "Robin Hood".

2.2 The Fiscal Responsibility System and Township Enterprises

Having noticed the impact of the relationship between the central government and local governments on the behaviors of the latter and China's economic growth, many scholars have devoted much time to furtherize empirical studies. It is revealed that the fiscal responsibility system has been a decentralized system from the perspective of the relationship between governments at the two levels since the mid-1980s, which has greatly promoted China's economic growth by means of fiscal decentralization-based regional competition. Lin Justin Yifu and Liu Zhiqiang validated the evident relation between the fiscal responsibility system and local economic growth based on available data at the provincial level in this phase. Others also reached a similar conclusion although they utilized different measurement indices.

Although it directly established the connection between fiscal decentralization and local economic growth, the quantitative analysis did not properly cover the underlying mechanism. The implicit mechanism behind such a connection was that fiscal decentralization encouraged the regional competition among local governments and gave impetus for promoting economic growth, and regional economic growth was indeed realized. The key to this mechanism lied in how fiscal decentralization stimulated local governments and how local governments enhanced economic growth. The first question has been answered in the above analysis, while the latter needs to be studied in depth. There are many approaches to promoting economic growth. Although it has been verified that fiscal decentralization could actually promote economic growth, the empirical study did not reveal how it was achieved, which, however, is vital to our understanding of their connection.

Some scholars believe that the answer is industrialization, especially the rise and prosperity of township-run enterprises. How did township-run enterprises become so successful? The academic circle has offered numerous answers. Bearing most distinct Chinese characteristics, township-run enterprises are mainly characterized by two features: (1) They were established in rural areas, rather than urban areas relatively more developed in terms of the performance of scale economy, and farmers entitled to land use constituted the main force; (2) They were owned by the township or village collectively, which is a common ownership structure. Township-run enterprises flourished in the 1980s and rapidly grew into a force at core in promoting China's economic development. Researchers discovered some characteristics of such enterprises from the perspective of ownership, and scholars held that the key to their success lied in the industrial structure, rather than the unique ownership structure. Jean C. Oi et al. put more emphasis on the positive role played by local governments in local industrialization and proposed the concept of "corporatism of local governments" in explaining the reasons behind the rise of township-run enterprises and local industrialization. She held that under the fiscal responsibility system established in the mid-1980s, local governments could obtain not only revenues beyond the responsibility base, but also extra-budget profits from turnover by township-run enterprises. And this played a significant role in stimulating the rise of township-run enterprises.

How did the increase in fiscal revenues stimulate the rise of township-run enterprises? This question should be answered based on a full understanding of the tax system. Since the substitution of tax payment for profit delivery in 1983, tax has become a major component of fiscal revenues. Thereby, it was the mass of not only budgetary fiscal revenues, but also the contractual base. The base did not provide percentages of different types of taxes, so a package contract should be adopted and maintained for several successive years. The greater the extra-base portion was, the more the retainable by local governments would become (in some regions, it was even 100% retainable). Therefore, the increasing rate of taxes was the key to satisfying or even over-fulfilling the base.

The tax system adopted the traditional classification method that had been implemented since the founding of the People's Republic of China. In this method, enterprises have been the major source of taxes. The business income tax and the turnover tax (mainly including the product tax and the value added tax as imposed later) have been classified in accordance with affiliation and territoriality, respectively. The turnover tax, as the major component under the tax system, should be equivalent to 2–4 times of the income tax in terms of value. In such a way, the industrial and commercial taxes and the fiscal revenues of local governments may be closely inter-connected. Therefore, the economic aggregate and fiscal revenues may both achieve rapid increase as long as local government-run enterprises proliferate.

The product tax has been the largest in amount among all items of industrial and commercial taxes. Since 1984, it has been imposed on almost all industrial products based on the sales gain, subject to the State's adjustment according to the positions of different products in the production/sales chain in view of inter-enterprise equity. The costs and profits of the enterprises should not be considered as it has been levied as per the sales gain. In 1986, China determined that some taxation items should be transferred from the scope of the product tax to that of the VAT as derived from the product tax, the number of which had increased to 174 as of April

1991, excluding only 86 items, such as cigarettes, alcohol, etc., among the 260 items of industrial products in total that were originally included in scope of the product tax. The calculation formula of the VAT is:

Tax to be paid by an ordinary taxpayer = current tax amount of offset items − current income tax amount.

As the VAT rate is fixed (17%), the tax payable should be equal to the product of this rate and the difference between sales gain and costs of raw materials. It corresponds to the value-added part, rather than products sales income. The product tax and the VAT, both included in the turnover tax, should be imposed on any in-operation or sales gain-producing enterprise (no matter profitable or not). The base of the VAT includes the costs of production and management, in addition to raw materials. The factory price would be certainly higher than the costs of raw materials, even if the enterprises are not profitable, because it includes the wages of workers, depreciation costs of production equipments, etc. In addition, the larger an enterprise is, the greater the turnover will be; as a result, the VAT and the product tax will be enhanced. Both items of taxation constitute the major part of not only the turnover tax, but also the total taxes. In the 1980s, the product tax and the VAT accounted for more than a third of the total tax revenues of China. However, the business income tax levied based on the net profit of enterprises accounted for only 19% of the total in 1991. Different from state-owned enterprises, township-run enterprises had been favored by relief policies before 1994, and allowed for various pre-tax profit distribution policies. This provided for tax avoidance and evasion. Therefore, high in value and easy in sales invoice-based collection as they might be, the product tax and the VAT should be attached with great significance in view of an opportunity for local governments to enhance their respective fiscal revenues.

A large proportion of the after-tax profits of township-run enterprises should be delivered to the government at the township or village level and included in extra-budgetary revenues. More specifically, the revenues of governments at the county, village and township levels were comprised by taxes payable by township-run enterprises, profits delivered by village-run enterprises, budgetary taxes shared with the county government, and extra-budgetary profits turned over by relevant enterprises. Therefore, the county government has been the most concerned about the size of township-run enterprises, rather than whether they were profitable or not, and in reality, the people's governments at the county level have always been the most efficient in facilitating access to credit.

The tax system and the fiscal responsibility system have greatly encouraged local governments to promote industrialization at the grassroots level. Under the tax system of the 1980s, the most direct and most effective approach to enhancing fiscal revenues was to establish local enterprises, and the product tax and the VAT payable by enterprises were the major components of increased fiscal revenues. From 1985 to 1991, the year-on-year increasing rates of total taxes, the product tax plus the VAT, and the business income tax were 7.7, 8 and 1.8%, respectively. The product tax and the VAT were related to the size of enterprises, while the business income tax was determined as per corporate profits. It can be seen that local industry, especially the rapid development of township-run enterprises, was an important impetus in promoting the growth of national fiscal revenues, which has however been scarcely associated with the performance of enterprises.

Since the late 1980s, besides the Pearl River Delta, the Yangtze River Delta and Zhejiang where vigorous development of township-run enterprises was witnessed, Shandong, Hebei, Liaoning, and some other provinces in Central China also have embarked on starting undertakings, and some areas even called on every village to start undertakings and every household to participate in such undertakings. Township-run enterprises in these areas were mostly financed by local governments-summoned banks, credit cooperatives, and rural cooperative foundations, and thus immediately brought about an increase in the GDP and fiscal revenues, no matter whether they were profitable or not.

2.3 The Fiscal Responsibility System and State-Owned Enterprises

Another significant role in the industrialization at the first stage of reform and opening up was played by state-owned enterprises. Different from the vigorously developing township-run enterprises, state-owned enterprises have progressively explored their reform, accompanied by complex institutional changes. It involved the enterprise fund system, the profit retention scheme, substitution of tax payment for profit delivery, the responsibility system, the shareholding system, etc. In general, the reform has been extended from profit distribution to the management system, and then to the property right system. The reform of the property rights system took place at the second stage of the reform and opening up, while that of profit distribution and the management system was mostly completed at the first stage.

It is worth noticing is that the reform of state-owned enterprises was quite different from the practices of delegating or retaking powers in enterprises management. The reform at this stage focused on enhancing vitality and transforming the operation mechanism of enterprises, rather than simply delegating jurisdiction and administration authorities to local governments. To this end, the reform of in-enterprise distribution and the tax system was accomplished under the condition that market economy had not yet been established.

Before the reform, the increased fiscal revenues of China sourced from profit delivery by enterprises, rather than taxes. In fact, under the solid planned economic system, there were great differences in profit margin among different industries and different enterprises, subject to the State's decision based on the prices of fixed assets, raw materials and products. So it was difficult to absorb the profits of enterprises via taxation. Less and less important as it became, taxation was even excluded from the fiscal approaches to socialism during the Cultural Revolution. As most of the tax items have been consolidated since the end of 1972, state-owned enterprises are now only subject to industrial and commercial taxes, and only 44 (of originally 108) items are retained. In 1972, taxes levied on enterprises accounted for only 41.4% of the fiscal revenues of China, which has been the lowest in history.

After being piloted in several areas, the substitution of tax payment for profit delivery was first implemented in two steps across the nation in 1983, and then further improved in 1985. The basic idea was substituting the payment of business income tax and regulatory income tax payable by state-owned enterprises for profit delivery to the State or competent organs. Large and medium-sized state-owned enterprises should pay the business income tax at 55%; and in case of any inter-enterprise difference in profit margin, the regulatory income tax should be imposed. After this policy was officially implemented, the proportion of enterprise profit delivery to total fiscal revenues experienced a continuous decline, dropping from 40% in 1980 to 1.9% in 1986; in contrast, during the same period, the proportion of tax revenues increased from 52.7 to 92.5%.

In 1987, the central government started the reform of the responsibility system for enterprises. During the 5th meeting of the National People's Congress dated in early 1987, it was proposed in the *Report on the Work of the Government* to carry out various forms of the contract magagerial responsibility system. By the end of 1987, 80% of large and medium-sized enterprises had completed the reform.

The responsibility system for enterprises was characterized by a fixed base and a guarantee for turnover to competent authorities. Under this system, any surplus/ deficit should be retained /made up by the enterprises. This idea was basically similar to the responsibility system with remuneration linked to output for rural areas and the fiscal contractual system implemented between the central government and local governments. However, as these enterprises were owned by the State and involved in organized production activities, and a real market economy had not been established yet, coupled with the administrative pricing behaviors influential on the business and profits of enterprises, the reform of the responsibility system for state-owned enterprises actually zigzagged (unlike that of the responsibility system with remuneration linked to output for rural areas), and the results cannot be evaluated in undiscriminately.

The responsibility system has undoubtedly played a significant role in enhancing enterprises' vitality and independence in their business; however, whether their economic performance has been promoted is still a question. As shown in Fig. 2.1, the margin of profits declined obviously upon the implementation of the responsibility system. Despite the various factors behind such a decline, its positive impacts on economic performance can hardly be found.

A direct cause behind the sharp drop in profit margins was the mushroom of fixed assets as well as the resulting increase in production costs, as can be easily seen from the above figure. From 1984 to 1984, the total fixed assets of industrial enterprises witnessed an annual average growth rate as high as 20%, while profits decreased to almost only 1/3 of the original amount.

The increase in taxes levied on enterprises was related to the substitution of tax payment for profit delivery and, more importantly, the significant changes of the entire tax system during the mid-1982s. Although the policy of substituting tax

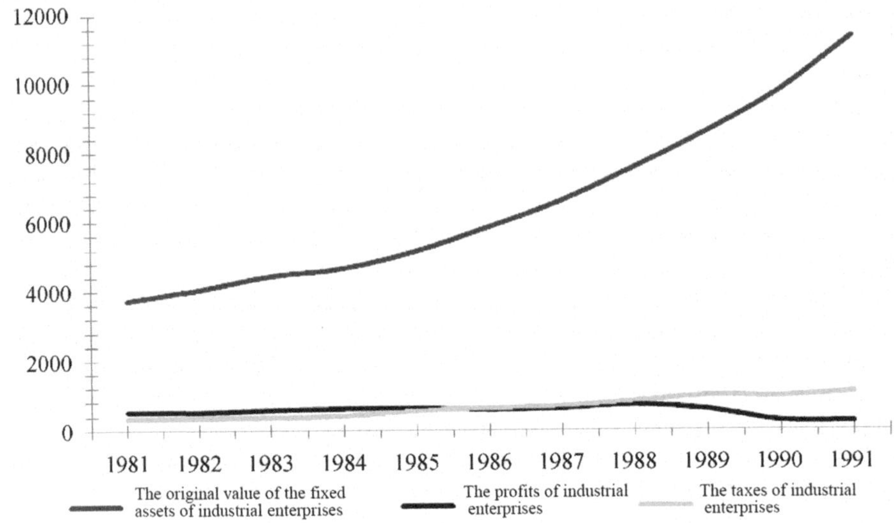

Fig. 2.1 Impact of the contract system on corporate profits (*unit* CNY 100 million). *Data source* Comprehensive planning department of the Ministry of Finance, ed., *Financial Statistics of China*, Beijing: Science Press, 1992

Table 2.1 Components of taxes levied on enterprises (Including the income tax and the turnover tax) (1985–1991) (*unit* CNY 100 million). *Data Source* Comprehensive planning department of the Ministry of Finance (ed.), *Financial Statistics of China*, Beijing: Science Press, 1992, p. 44

Year	Business income tax	Regulatory tax	Subtotal	Tax on products	VAT	Business tax	Subtotal
1985	513.8	82.04	595.84	594.6	147.7	211.07	953.37
1986	523.67	71.73	595.4	546.59	232.19	261.07	1039.85
1987	505.25	57.95	563.2	533.26	254.2	302	817.46
1988	514.54	56.39	570.93	480.93	384.37	397.92	1263.22
1989	519.21	64.38	583.59	530.28	430.83	487.3	1448.41
1990	543.1	61.02	604.12	580.93	400	515.75	1496.68
1991				629.41	406.36	564	1599.77

payment (including the business income tax and the regulatory income tax imposed on state-owned enterprises) for profit delivery had been influential on revenues growth, the profit-based taxes did not increase obviously as a result of the decline of profit margins in industrial enterprises, which is demonstrated by the Table 2.1.

From the table above, it can be seen that the income tax hardly increased from 1985 to 1990, suggesting that the growth of taxes levied on enterprises was not driven by the income growth. In contrast, the turnover tax achieved an annual average growth rate as high as 11.3%, playing a significant role to this end.

It can be seen from the analysis above that the expansion of fixed assets was accompanied by the growth of the turnover tax, but un-correlated to the increase of the income tax and even negatively correlated to the profits obtained by enterprises. Most items of the turnover tax were based on the output value or added value which were directly related to the size of enterprises. Under the fiscal responsibility system, the major approach for competent authorities or local governments to enhancing fiscal revenues and the GDP should be business expansion, rather than income promotion.

Thus, we can see the relationship between local governments and state-owned enterprises under the fiscal contractual system has experienced a basically similar evolution to that between the contractual system and township-run enterprises: business expansion was a major focus for local governments, attached with priority over the financial performance of enterprises and the GDP/fiscal revenues of local governments. The operation of the responsibility system for state-owned enterprises has also promoted the shaping of this situation. This was mainly related to the design of two key subsystems under the responsibility system.

One was the tax-inclusive contract subsystem, whereby the base quota included the business income tax and the regulatory income tax payable by the enterprises. It lasted from 1987 when the responsibility system was first implemented across the nation to 1993. Under this subsystem, the income tax should be paid at a rate of 55% lower than the base in case of any profits higher than the base quota, and should the income tax and the regulatory tax exceed the base quota, excessive taxes would be returned to the enterprises. In such a way, the business income tax and the regulatory income tax may be cut down as long as the actual output exceeded the base quota; and the greater the excess was, the less the actual tax payment would be. Thus the tax-inclusive contract became actually a tax-cutting contract. With a claim to both the income tax and the regulatory tax, local governments should never relay on the income tax to enhance their respective fiscal revenues.

The other was the pre-tax repayment subsystem, whereby any loan should be deducted prior to the calculation of the income tax. This played two roles in practice. On the one hand, similar to that of the tax-inclusive contract system, it reduced the actual payment of the income tax. The bigger the increased loans were, the more would be deducted from the income tax. On the other hand, it actually encouraged the enterprises to increase their respective loans, because the increased profits from investment with such loans were spared from paying the income tax. Local governments had been highly motivated to help the enterprises to obtain new loans, for the investment with new loans may directly enhance the tax on products, VAT, business tax and other turnover taxes, as calculated based on the output value. This has led to a rapid business expansion with the support of new loans. From 1986 to 1990, bank loans granted to local enterprises increased from CNY 269.309 billion to CNY 668.377 billion, with an annual increasing rate of 37%.

The expansion of bank loans and the total fixed assets had led to a sharp decline of profit margins on the one hand and a rapid growth of tax payment by the enterprises on the other. It was the result of the interaction between the fiscal responsibility system and the responsibility system for enterprises. Under the latter system, the proportion of retentions by enterprises increased sharply, while payment of the income tax and the regulatory tax was basically maintained steady; under the former system, local governments and enterprises jointly promoted a continuous business expansion. This has played a significant role in the evolution of the relationship between the central government and local governments.

2.4 Impact of the Responsibility System on the Relationship Between the Central Government and Local Governments

The fiscal responsibility system has been closely related to the rise of township-run enterprises and the reform of state-owned enterprises. It can be seen from the foregoing analysis that under the stimulus of the fiscal responsibility system, local governments and local enterprises have gradually become an interests community. Based on a comparison with the situation prior to the reform, we can easily capture the following changes.

Firstly, the administration system fragmented by regional autonomy and vertical control or dominated by the latter has gradually become dominated by the former. Unlike the changes procured by the central government through directly delegating administration over enterprises and vital materials to local governments during the Great Leap Forward and the Cultural Revolution, this was achieved with the help of fiscal contracting, based on negotiations between the central government and local governments. Considering the obvious difference in the economic situation among different regions, various contract bases and surplus retention methods were adopted. Negotiations went held almost every year between the central government and local governments and/or between different local governments. Thus, the interest boundary of each concerned party was gradually defined. It is found in a study that the bargaining chip of local governments during such negotiations was the local economic development, and a basic logic of recurring to the fiscal responsibility system in view of local economic development was established, which helped local governments to obtain subjective consciousness gradually.

Secondly, in the interaction among the central government, local governments and local enterprises, the central government gradually abandoned its direct administration over enterprises via subordinate departments and thus became the trustor of local governments and enterprises. The reform of the tax system and the implementation of the responsibility system for enterprises also made local governments the trustor of enterprises and thus no more directly intervene with the production, operation and distribution of the enterprises. To a certain extent, this has achieved separation of government functions from enterprise management. However, under the increasing pressure from the fiscal responsibility system, local governments and local enterprises were closely correlated to each other in interests and thus formed an interests community. Despite their renouncement of direct intervention with enterprises, local governments basically relied on enhancing the turnover tax by taking initiative to help enterprises obtain bank loans and thus achieve rapid enhancement of fixed assets and production scale, so as to accomplish their respective targets under the fiscal responsibility system. For enterprises, the expansion in fact made the enterprises a trump card, for they have become local governments' own business. Therefore, any loss of an enterprise would be covered by its competent local government. Meanwhile, the responsibility system for enterprises also provided an institutional guarantee for enhancing the retention proportion and even cutting down the income tax.

Finally, although significant changes had occurred to the relationship between the central government and local governments, and the latter had turned from direct intervention to facilitation-based stimulation, there were still obvious differences from a real market economy. By facilitation-based stimulation, it means local governments mobilized local resources by various administrative or semi-administrative facilitation approaches for the sake of business expansion, rather than by establishing a real market mechanism whereby enterprises may truly enhance their vitality in market competition. In fact, under the double-track pricing system (characterized by the co-existence of planned prices and market prices), on the one hand, enterprises became more prone to rent-seeking in their pursuit of business expansion; on the other hand, local governments were further inclined to rent-providing with the view of enhancing their revenues. Although both the local GDP and fiscal revenues might be rapidly enhanced in such a situation, local governments and enterprises had gone against market economy. In such a development model, local governments actually took a greater part in the interests chain and thus became more closely connected with the fate of enterprises, despite of its exit from business management. For state-owned enterprises, the loans, liquidity and profits of enterprises were basically all under the control of local governments. This contributed to the situation where loans granted to enterprises by banks had to be repaid from fiscal revenues of the competent government. Moreover, enterprises run by townships became even more closely related to and were virtually equivalent to those run by local governments.

The aforesaid changes were caused by the devolution of powers. In turn, the relationship between the central government and local governments were also affected. Local governments gradually obtained independent interests and strengthened their domination over the increased economic resources during their close interaction with local enterprises. It had directly led to a reduced control over the re-distribution by the central government and a tension between the central government and local governments.

According to the study of the academic circle, two proportions decreased sharply under the fiscal responsibility system, namely the proportion of fiscal revenues to the GDP and the proportion of fiscal revenues of the central government to total fiscal revenues. The following is a careful analysis of these two proportions.

The proportion of fiscal revenues to the GDP corresponds to the revenues obtained from economic growth by means of taxation and charging. It is a reflection of the State control over redistribution by fiscal means. Generally speaking, taxes and charges are the major components of budgetary and extra-budgetary fiscal revenues, respectively. The calculated proportion of budgetary fiscal revenues to the GDP and that of total fiscal revenues (budgetary revenues plus extra-budgetary revenues) to the GDP were as shown in the Fig. 2.2.

The variation amplitudes of the two curves as shown in the above figure are basically identical. The proportion of budgeted fiscal revenues to the GDP decreased from 24% in 1981 to 12.3% in 1993, and that of total fiscal revenues to the GDP also decreased from 36% in 1981 to 27.2% in 1992, and then to 16.4% in 1993, as a result of a sharp drop of extra budgeted revenues.

The second to be analyzed is the proportion of centrally controlled fiscal revenues to the total fiscal revenues. The proportions of fiscal revenues and expenditures of the central government to total fiscal revenues and expenditures

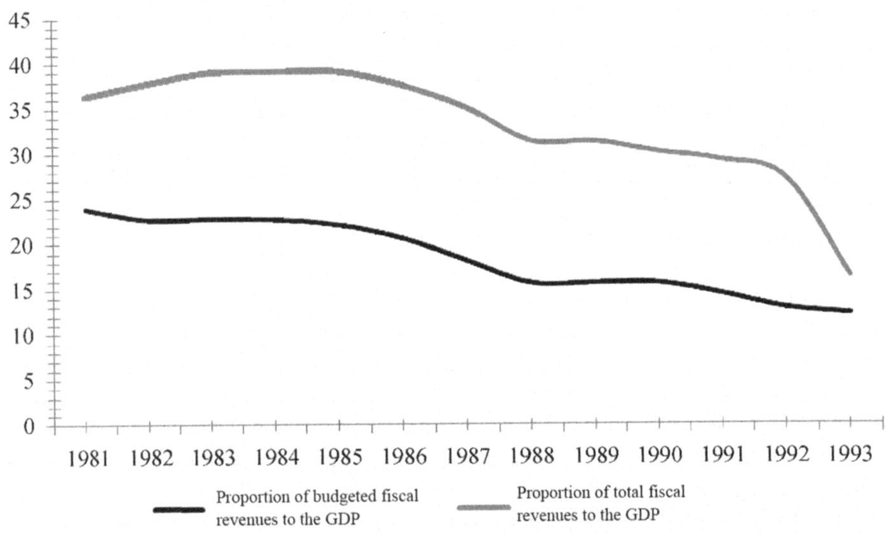

Fig. 2.2 Proportion of budgeted fiscal revenues to the GDP and proportion of total fiscal revenues (budgeted revenues plus extra budgeted revenues) to the GDP. *Data source* China monthly economic indicators publishing house, ed., *30 years of digital China—A compilation of statistical data for the 30 years since the reform and opening up*; Budget department of the Ministry of Finance, ed., *Statistical Data of Local Finance of China* (1999), Beijing: China Financial & Economic Publishing House, 1999

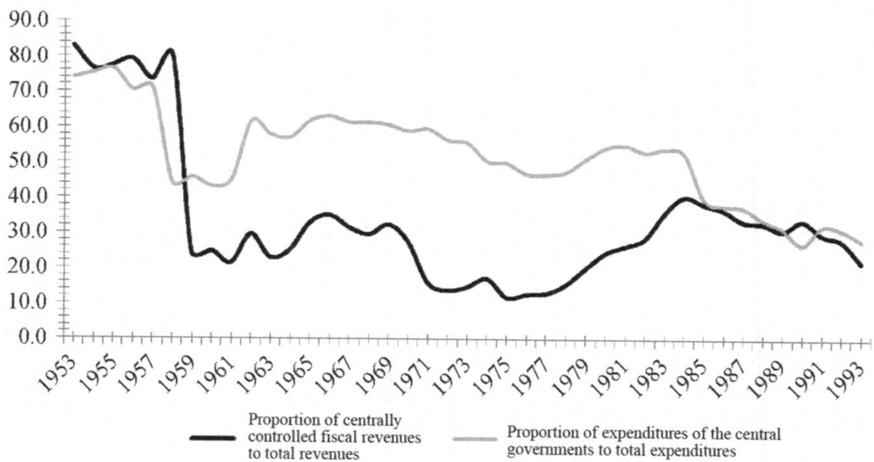

Fig. 2.3 Proportions of fiscal revenues and expenditures of the central governments to total revenues and expenditures respectively (1953–1993). *Data source* Lou Jiwei, ed., *Fiscal statistics for the 50 years since the founding of the PRC*, Beijing: Economic Science Press, 2000

respectively are listed in order to better understand the impact of the fiscal responsibility on their variations, and the time frame is extended to prior to the reform, as shown in the Fig. 2.3.

As shown in the figure above, the proportions of centrally controlled fiscal revenues to the total decreased significantly from 40.5% in 1984 to 22% in 1993. However, when put in a longer time frame, the proportions during this period were obviously not the lowest, but higher than those from 1959 to 1980. The control of the central government over redistribution, if understood based on these data, was still more centralized compared with the situation before the reform and opening up, despite of a slight decline. This was obviously to the opposite of the general course. Another key to the understanding of the situation is the proportion of fiscal expenditures of the central government to total fiscal expenditures.

Prior to the reform and opening up, there was a sharp difference between the low proportion of centrally controlled fiscal revenues and the quite high proportion of fiscal expenditures of the central government. It indicates that a large portion of fiscal revenues obtained by local governments were turned over to the central government for spending. Since the mid-1980s, there has been quite a turn-round as the central government has basically maintained a balance between revenues and expenditures. This avoided the necessity to cover the high expenditures with the large-volume turnover by local governments. Thus, retentions might be made to cover their respective expenditures. In short, the fiscal responsibility system has helped the central government and local governments to maintain their respective balance of fiscal revenues and expenditures.

As local governments were independently responsible for their respective revenues and expenditures, the proportions of fiscal revenues and expenditures of the central government decreased, while those of local governments witnessed a gradual creeping-up. This was mainly because a majority of the increment of State revenues was retained by local governments under the fiscal responsibility system. Based on the statistics for the period from 1984 to 1993, we can obtain:

Centrally controlled fiscal revenues = CNY 50.9 billion + 0.12 $\times$ total fiscal revenues.

That is to say, every additional CNY 1 would be split between the central government and local governments as per CNY 0.12 versus 0.88. If this trend has continued, the proportion of centrally controlled fiscal revenues would continue to fall; and the responsibility system spared local governments from turnover to the central government. So, the proportion of expenditures would not witness any increase. This was basically why the central government attempted to substitute the tax-sharing system for the fiscal responsibility system.

Chapter 3
Tax-Sharing System

The tax-sharing system carried out by the central government in 1994 may be regarded as a blanket dismissal of the fiscal responsibility system. As a brand-new fiscal reform, it not only embodied the efforts made by the central government to adjust its relationship between local governments and enterprises, but also its attempt to thoroughly transform direct governmental economic intervention into a comprehensive socialist market economy. At present, the academia usually try to study the tax-sharing system from the perspective of the relationship between the central government and local governments. For instance, according to Wang Shaoguang, under the fiscal responsibility system, local governments accumulated substantial financial capabilities, while the central government shared only a tiny part of fiscal revenues, an embodiment of the early stage of a fragmented economy. This not only curtailed the central government's ability to adjust and control economical operation, but also damaged its authority. Against such a background, the tax-sharing system was a demand inevitable for centralization.

As a matter of fact, China encountered great fiscal difficulties after the fiscal responsibility system had been implemented for nearly ten years. Fiscal revenues could not be amassed by the central government any longer like it had been, and both the central government and local governments had to rely on their own revenues to cover their expenditures. However, the new increase of fiscal revenues was mostly sourced from local finance, resulting in an inevitable sharp decline in the fiscal share of the central government. Such fiscal difficulties impelled the central government to change the fiscal and taxation systems. This was one of the reasons for implementing the tax-sharing system. The implementation of the system was related to the economic situation of that time and the government-enterprises relationship.

F. Zhou and M. Tan, *Relationship between the Central Government and Local Governments of Contemporary China*, Social Development Experiences in China,
DOI 10.1007/978-981-10-4388-8_3

Following the economic downturn caused by the blockage of international trade of 1989, Deng Xiaoping's talks in the South (1992), which was aimed at an accelerated transition from planned economy to market economy, started a new round of economic construction. Convened in October, the 14th NPC proposed to build a socialist market economy. Piloted by local governments, there was a rapid increase of investment and township-run enterprises, coupled with nationwide efforts to accelerate the reform of the responsibility system and share-holding system for state-owned enterprises. The quotation of Shanghai Stock Exchange increased by 1200% during the first half of 1992, while Shenzhen Stock Exchange experienced a turbulence in August, 1992, resulting in a two-day-long total paralysis of the city. The economic growth before the economic downturn was immediately recovered, reaching 14.2% in 1992 and 14% in 1993 (compared with 4.1% in 1989, 3.8% in 1990 and 9.2% in 1991), the highest in the 1990s, or even in the 30 years following the reform and opening up.

Despite the rapid economic growth during this period, the government-led local and investment expansion-driven growth pattern had been continued, which further promoted the interaction between local governments and enterprises under the fiscal responsibility system, rather than the establishment of a market economy. The most important target of local governments in their efforts to stimulate the increase of enterprises was to accelerate GDP growth, in response to Deng Xiaoping's talks in the South. Many rural areas were also required by the government to start local business and provide working opportunities to each household. National investment in fixed assets achieved a year-on-year growth by 44% in 1992 and 62% in 1993, of which the major component, namely domestic loans, increased by 68 and 39% respectively, which was really rare during the 30 years following the reform and opening up. This was one of the major engines that promoted economic growth.

This government-led economic growth pattern was, to a great extent, another version of the government administration pattern in the planned economy. It can be deduced from the analysis in the previous two chapters that the economic development just turned from a pattern dominated by regional administration by local governments to one fragmented by vertical control as well as regional administration. The situation prior to the reform and opening up could be considered as a fragmented pattern, while that under the fiscal responsibility system was typically dominated by regional administration. The central government relied on accelerating devolution and encouraging inter-local-government competitions to realize economic development. Therefore, the interests of local governments and those of enterprises became even more closely inter-connected. The excessive investment soon brought about various issues such as redundant constructions, regional protectionism, etc., just like the situation incurred by the economic boom in previous times. Despite of its incentive effect on economic growth, the local government-led pattern stimulated the development of market economy based on the market rather than administrative resources allocation.

So the reasons for implementing tax-sharing system are: (1) the awkward situation confronting state revenues in the relationship between the central government and local governments; (2) the complicated relationship between governments and enterprises. The fiscal responsibility system could not achieve a separation of governments and enterprises. Instead, it aggravated their interactions to a certain degree which, in turn, hampered the fiscal capabilities of the central governments. These two reasons inevitably brought about centralization under the tax-sharing system as well as a profound influence on the government-enterprises relationship.

3.1 Background and Basic Connotations of the Tax-Sharing System

Broadly speaking, the tax-sharing system-based reform may be divided into two parts, namely, the tax reform aimed at re-determination and adjustment of tax categories and the reform of the fiscal system aimed at a re-division of fiscal and administrative authority between the central government and local governments as well as its necessary adjustment. Let's begin our analysis with a review of the tax reform.

The reform of the tax system mainly included the following moves:

The first and foremost was the reform of turnover taxes, whereby the VAT (Value Added Tax) excluding price was levied uniformly at 17% in the processes of production and circulation in place of the complicated tax on products. In addition to the VAT, a consumption duty was imposed on a few consumer goods. The scope of the business tax was also adjusted. The new scope mainly covered 9 industries subject to 3 tax rates.

The second was the reform of the income tax. The business income tax was levied on uniform tax categories at a uniform rate (33%) based on a single tax setting standard, in place of the different tax policies differentiating state-owned enterprises, collective enterprises and private enterprises, where the policy of pre-tax loan repayment was canceled. The personal income tax was also imposed uniformly.

Finally, some other taxes (such as the resource tax) were adjusted, and the land value increment tax was also levied.

The reformed aspects of the fiscal system of the central government and local governments were as following:

Firstly, fiscal revenues were shared between the central government and local governments as per taxation items based on the allocation of their respective expenditure responsibilities. In such a context, the taxes were divided into three categories, namely central taxes, local taxes and shared taxes. The first category mainly included consumption duty, tariff, excise and VAT levied by the CIQ on delivery, central enterprises income tax, major taxes (including business tax, income tax, profit tax and city maintenance construction tax) to be paid by entities under the Ministry of Railways, head offices of banks, insurance companies, etc., and profits delivered by central enterprises. The second category included business tax, income tax and profits to be handed over to the state by local enterprises, personal income tax, and other minor items. The general principle was that central enterprises taxes should be paid to the central government, while those payable to local governments could be retained by local governments, except the VAT, resource tax, and transfer tax on stock. And the third category included the VAT (75% payable to the central government, and 25% retainable for local governments), resource tax (taxes on offshore petroleum resources to be paid to the central government, others retainable for local governments) and transfer tax on stock (50–50 shared by the central government and local governments).

Secondly, tax rebates and the transfer payment system were adopted. In order to enhance major tax-paying provinces' enthusiasm for developing business and maintaining the distribution pattern of vested interests, the tax-sharing system stipulated the means of rebating taxes. The tax rebates were based on the statistics of 1993. The net turnover to the central government (namely 75% of the VAT + consumption duty—revenues allocated to governments at lower levels by the central government) from the VAT and consumption duty, originally the major sources of taxes revenues of local governments, should be fully returned to local governments. And increments were returned as per 1:0.3 of the average increase rate of each region's turnover to the central government from the VAT and consumption duty so as to kindle their enthusiasm in helping the central government collecting taxes. Two years after the implementation of the tax-sharing system, the central government further introduced the policy of transfer payment during the transitional period, whereby it should use part of the increased revenues to mainly address the key issues encountered in local fiscal operation based on the pre-determined amount of subsidy for transfer payment, giving considerations to the objective factors and policy elements that had a relatively direct impact on local fiscal revenues and expenditures as well as the fiscal efforts made by local governments, and proper priority was given to regions inhabited by ethnic groups. These two policies were aimed at an inter-regional adjustment of financial resources in view of both maintaining developed regions' enthusiasm for collecting taxes and transferring a part of the tax revenues to poorer regions in pursuit of equalization under the fiscal system.

Thirdly, two sets of taxation institutions were established. One set was administrated by the central government, the other the local governments. Two sets of institutions collected taxes independently. Meanwhile, the governance-based taxation method applied to enterprises was preliminarily modified. According to the design of the tax-sharing system, all major items of taxation (including the VAT, consumption duty and business income tax) should be allocated according to the classification method of the tax-sharing system. In contrast to the previous interwinding of tax and finance of local governments, this reform brought about an independent tax system under vertical control, whereby local tax departments should be responsible for the department of taxation at a higher level. Tax departments were directly regulated by the SAT, which guaranteed a continuous increase of not only central revenues along with the locally obtained part, but also the proportion of fiscal revenues to the GDP in pace with local economic development.

It can be concluded from the analysis above that the tax-sharing system was undoubtedly a fiscal reform launched by the central government. The reform was characterized by the centralization of fiscal revenues obtained by local governments and the authority over taxation and expenditure responsibilities.

First of all, as a result of the separation of finance and tax, the power of taxation was centralized. Before the reform, taxation functioned as a sector under the financial system, while the financial sector was actually the money bag of local governments, which ought to be controlled most stringently. For their benefits, local governments might manipulate taxation so as to "hide wealth in enterprises". Besides the pre-tax loan payment under the enterprise contract and responsibility system, tax relief and other preferential policies were introduced, leading to a continuous expansion of the scope of tax relief. Some regions even reduced and remitted taxes beyond their authority. According to a survey on industrial and commercial tax relief in 10 provinces/municipalities conducted by the National Audit Office, the turnover tax relief reached CNY 9.7 billion in 1990, accounting for 20.7% of the total payment of turnover taxes; in 1991, 19 provinces were found with unauthorized tax relief, which accounted for 22.7% of the total amount concerning violation of discipline. In addition, tax evasion was quite common among local governments. A survey conducted in a certain province revealed that 70% of state-run enterprises, 72% of collective enterprises, and 85.5% of individual and private sectors of the economy were involved in tax evasion.

Under the tax-sharing system, taxes were unequivocally divided into three categories, namely, central taxes, local taxes and tax revenue shared by the central and local governments. The tax legislation power deciding the first and the third categories and some vital items included in the second category belonged to the central government. Moreover, the powers over adjustment of rates of major tax items, levy or cessation and approval of tax relief were also centralized. This situation was correlated with the separation of finance and tax. As tax departments were under the direct jurisdiction of the State Tax Administration, regional administration was replaced by vertical control. The staff, their salaries, equipments and business of the tax departments were all under the administration of a higher authority and thus separated from local finance. These adjustments to the fiscal system guaranteed the relative independence of tax departments from the local fiscal system and the implementation/execution of pertinent tax policies at the grass-roots level.

Second, that tax revenues were centralized at the central government was the most outstanding effect of the tax-sharing system. Now see the Fig. 3.1.

As demonstrated in the figure above, the centrally controlled proportions of state revenue before and after 1994 are in sharp contrast, which was basically caused by the fact that the VAT and consumption duty were divided into central taxes and shared taxes. In 1994, these two items reached CNY 308.97 billion, accounting for 53.6% of the fiscal revenues of the year, including CNY 230.83 billion of VAT, which was almost half of the total state revenue. This was the major reason for the rapid increase of the centrally controlled proportion of state revenue.

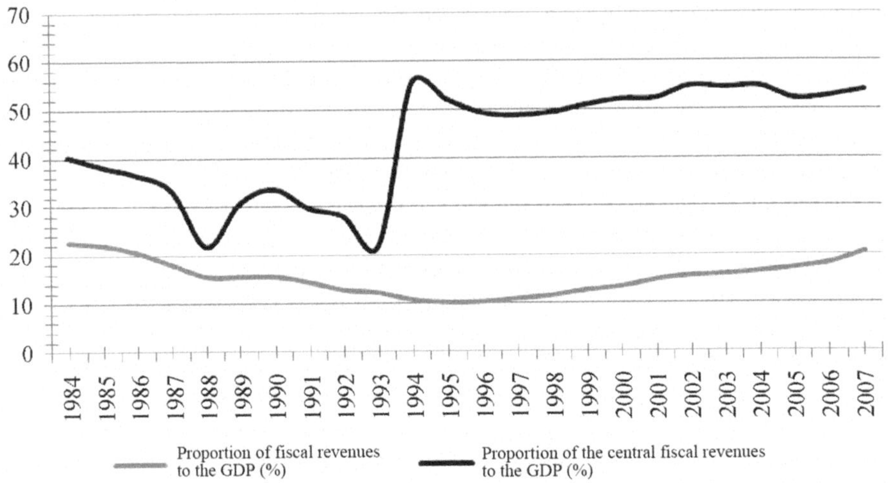

Fig. 3.1 Variation of the "Two Proportions". 财政收入占GDP (%): Proportion of fiscal revenues to the GDP (%). 中央财政收入占总收入 (%): Proportion of the central fiscal revenues to the GDP (%).

The central government intended to modify the responsibility "commitment" under the responsibility system to centralize local revenues, which was inevitably resisted by local governments. However, under the pressure from the central government, the modification was after all recognised across the country in a few months, revealing the absolute authority of the central government over local governments. Furthermore, the acceptance had much to do with the way of negotiating and compromising between governments at the two levels. The concession made by the central government was embodied by two aspects of the tax-sharing system, both of which were related to design of the tax rebates. As for the rebate of two taxes (the VAT and consumption duty), one design was based on the statistics of 1993, while the other was that the returned amount should increase in proportion to the increment of the VAT and consumption duty as per 1:0.3 (the central government: local governments) since 1994.

According to the design of the tax-sharing system, in 1994, the central government should return all the VAT and consumption duty to local governments according to the total sum of the two taxes in 1993 (base of tax rebates). Therefore, the sum of these two items in 1993 became the key factor that had a direct impact on the distribution of tax revenues between the central government and local governments. As the negotiations on the tax-sharing system between the central government and local governments took place in the second half of 1993, the final amount of taxes of 1993 had not been worked out yet, hence local governments could try their best to maximize the final sum of the VAT and consumption duty of the year of 1993. Realizing that local governments would try all means to enlarge the total sum of the total tax revenues of 1993 so as to increase the local rebate base, the Ministry of Finance advised to take the revenues of 1992 as the base of tax rebates. However, local governments insisted that the total sum of tax revenues of 1993 should be used as the rebate base as a condition of their support for the tax-sharing system.

This design in line with the interests of local governments resulted in an usually reaction of the tax revenues of the whole nation in 1993. The state revenues of 1993 achieved a year-on-year increase by 24.8%, which was indeed abnormal in view of the fact that the average growth rate of the previous five years was only 9.6%. This was nothing less than the result of the rapid growth of local revenues, for the centrally controlled revenues of 1993 witnessed a year-on-year decline by CNY 1.2 billion, while the absolute amount of local revenues increased by CNY 88.75 billion, 35% higher than that of the previous year.

In order to increase their revenues and thus enhance the base of tax rebates, local governments resorted to plenty of means. For instance, enterprises that had been covered by tax relief were required to make it up in order to raise the base of tax rebates, while the makeup was then reimbursed the enterprises under the counter. Taxes of bankrupt enterprises or long-standing defaulters were paid via bank transfer or loans. Other manipulations such as deficit spending and over-tax were not uncommon, too. The phenomena revealed the existence of local protectionism and the wealth hidden in local regions under the fiscal responsibility system, as well as the fact that the adoption of the data of 1993 as the base of tax rebates was actually a compromise made by the central government in view of the interests of local governments.

The other design of the tax-sharing system required that tax rebates should be calculated as per 1:0.3 based on the growth rate of the VAT and consumption duty, which was an embodiment of considerations given to the vested interests of local governments by the central government following fiscal centralization. However, the actual situation was far more complicated than simply adopting the tax revenue of 1993 as the base.

According to the original design of the tax-sharing system, the formula below should be used to calculate the tax rebates:

$$\begin{aligned}\text{Tax rebates} = {} & \text{refund of VAT and consumption duty in the previous year} \\ & \times (1 + \text{tax increment of the year VAT and consumption} \\ & \quad \text{as paid in the previous year}) \times 0.3.\end{aligned}$$

The "tax increment of the year/VAT and consumption as paid in the previous year" in the formula refers to the growth rate of the two taxes. The growth rate was calculated based on the average growth rate of the two items. Both the molecule and the denominator were their respective total amounts as collected nationwide rather than the actual growth rate of a certain region. This was obviously adverse to the interest of developed areas as the two items of taxation there increased rapidly. This standard benefited under-developed provinces. In July, 1994, the Ministry of Finance convened a symposium attended by the chiefs of the bureaus of finance of 11 provinces to modify the design. The average growth rate of the state in the formula for calculating the growth rate of the two taxes was replaced by the growth rate of a certain province, reflecting the considerations given to the vested interests of developed provinces by the central government.

Surprisingly, this 1:0.3 based design was totally unfavorable to local governments in the long run. As 100% of the consumption duty should be paid to the central government, we only need to calculate the VAT. Assuming the VAT of a certain province in 1993 amounted to CNY 10 billion, with an annual growth rate of 20%, the growth rate of income tax rebates would be 6% based on Formula (2). The proportion of such income tax rebates to the total tax revenue of the aforesaid province would diminish with time, that is, from 88% in 1994 to 54% in 1998, and then 29% ten years later. In fact, the proportion of tax rebates increment dropped obviously, so was that of locally shared proportion of the VAT (25% of the increment + rebate from increment), which was caused by the determination of 1:0.3, whereby the centrally controlled part was in the majority, as well as the fact that the proportion of the base of 1993 to tax rebates became increasingly negligible with the continuous rise of the total tax revenue. If calculated based on a growth rate of 20%, the base amount would only account for 16% of the total tax revenue ten years later. In 1997, the Ministry of Finance resolved to make it up to the national average by granting an annual subsidy of over CNY 0.3 billion to provincial units that had suffered sharp decline in tax rebates. From the above analysis, we can see that this design seemingly favored local governments at the beginning of the reform, but in the long run, the centrally controlled revenues actually obtained a substantial increase. Nevertheless, fiscal centralization was finally realized by the central government by means of introducing the tax-sharing system.

The analysis above has unveiled how centralization was achieved under the tax-sharing system. The mode of centralization differs from the so-called "chaos upon devolution of authority and stagnation upon re-taking it" prior to the reform. It was achieved by the re-taking of administrative authority over the enterprises or the direct turnover of locally obtained fiscal revenues, this was based on a re-determination of the respective scopes of taxation of the central government and local governments, showing significant changes in its approach to centralization. In addition, it cannot be considered as a complete fiscal centralization under the tax-sharing system in a strict sense. It was the centralization of financial authority or revenues, for the allocation of fiscal expenditure responsibilities was spared from material adjustment, maintaining 30:70 between the central government and local governments.

3.2 Tax-Sharing System and Transfer Payment System

From the analysis above, we know that the tax-sharing system was aimed at changing the relationship between the central government and local governments and that between the government and enterprises with the view of maintaining the central government's dominance as well as a continuous increase of the state revenues in the wake of the industrialization and prosperity of enterprises. In addition, the fiscal centralization could enable the central government to re-take the control over the re-adjustment and re-distribution of per capita resources, which would help to maintain an inter-regional balance of financial resources by gradually reducing the inter-regional differences, and thus achieve the goal of equalizing per capita fiscal expenditure. This may be regarded as one of the most important expenditure liabilities of the central government of a modern state. In order to achieve the goal, the key task for the central government upon the centralization of financial resources was to establish an effective and impartial fiscal transfer payment system.

Under the tax-sharing system, in contrast with the centralization of revenues was the fact that expenditure liabilities of the central government and local governments were spared from substantial adjustment, resulting in the abortion of the self-control of revenues and expenditures by governments at both levels under the fiscal responsibility system. In such a context, local governments were confronted with a huge fiscal gaps that could only be filled with the transfer payment of the central government, which was the most noticeable in the fiscal relationship between the central government and local governments since the implementation of the tax-sharing system.

The central government's transfer payment to local governments included three categories: tax rebates, special transfer payments and financial transfer payment. The first category refers to the rebates from the base and increment of the VAT and consumption duty under the tax-sharing system and, as a result of the reform of income tax increment sharing of 2002, from the base of income tax (including business income tax and personal income tax). Special transfer payment corresponded to the funds appropriated to local governments by the central government for designated purposes, commonly known as "predefined" funds. Other transfer payments by the central government are all referred to as financial transfer payments, appropriated by the central government to cover the expenditures of local governments.

From 1994 to 2005, the amounts of the three categories of transfer payments were as follows (Table 3.1).

The table shows that before 2000, tax rebates constituted the majority or more than half of the transfer payment. In 2005, each of the three categories accounted for a third of the total amount. The special transfer payment had increased significantly ever since 1997, while financial transfer payment did not upsoar until 2000, which was closely related to the central government's intention of adjusting its relationship with local governments as well as the behaviors of the latter.

Since 2002, the tax rebates have covered the rebates as per bases of four items of taxation and the rebates of the increments of the VAT. There was a noticeable increase of tax rebates ever since 2002 resulted from the base rebates of business income tax and personal income tax. The financial transfer payment, complicated in its various categories as it has been, is mainly aimed at encouraging local governments to provide equalized public services. In such a context, financial transfer payment would be intensively injected into the areas confronted with greater fiscal

Table 3.1 Amounts of three categories of transfer payments (1994–2005)

Year	Financial transfer payment		Special transfer payment		Tax rebates (VAT + consumption duty + income tax)		Total
	CNY 1 billion	%	CNY 1 billion	%	CNY 1 billion	%	CNY 1 billion
1994	9.9	4.4	36.1	16.0	179.9	79.6	225.9
1995	13.3	5.6	37.5	15.8	186.7	78.6	237.5
1996	16.1	6.2	48.9	18.8	194.9	75.0	259.9
1997	19.9	7.3	51.8	19.0	201.2	73.7	272.9
1998	21.0	6.6	87.8	27.7	208.3	65.7	317.1
1999	36.4	9.3	142.4	36.4	212.4	54.3	391.2
2000	62.0	14.0	161.3	36.3	220.7	49.7	444.0
2001	117.6	20.7	220.0	38.7	230.9	40.6	568.5
2002	162.3	22.1	240.1	32.7	332.8	45.3	735.2
2003	191.4	23.2	259.8	31.4	374.9	45.4	826.1
2004	260.5	25.0	342.3	32.9	438.0	42.1	1040.8
2005	381.2	33.2	352.9	30.7	414.3	36.1	1148.4

Data source Li Ping, *An Illustrated Interpretation of the Inter-government Fiscal Relationship in China*, Beijing: China Financial & Economic Publishing House, 2006; China State Finance Magazine, ed., *Finance Year Book of China* (2003–2006), Beijing: China State Finance Magazine, 2003–2006.

difficulties. In particular, the general transfer payment was established in 1995 with a view to realizing inter-regional fiscal equality. The payment was initially named as "transitional transfer payment" and later renamed as the "general transfer payment" since 2002. Mostly comprised of ordinary transfer payment, it also contained a small number of transfer payments to areas inhabited by ethnic minorities, old revolutionary base areas and border areas. Principally based on the regional fiscal revenues and expenditures, the ordinary transfer payment may be calculated as per the formula below:

$$(\text{Standard Expenditures of a Certain Region} - \text{Standard Revenues of the Region}) \\ \times \text{Payment Coefficient of the Region} = \text{Ordinary Transfer Payment of the Region.}$$

The standard expenditure and revenues should be calculated as per the numerous indicators promulgated by the central government. For instance, in 2005, revenues were calculated based on 48 indicators, including tax, corporate profits, wages, output of vital resources, etc., while expenditures based on 29 indicators, such as population, air temperature, agricultural acreage, grain yield, gasoline price, operating expense, completed region of the city, social security expenditure and so on and so forth. The sources of indicators were very complicated, including relevant state ministries and commissions, final accounts, *China Statistical Yearbook*, and pertinent statistical yearbooks on civil administration, municipalities, labor, rural areas, etc. The coefficient should be based on the total ordinary transfer payment divided by the local standard balance, a reflection of the gap between locally obtained revenues and expenditures covered by the central government by transfer payment. Following the income tax-sharing based reform of 2002, as the centralization of financial resources evolved, the equalization-pursuing ordinary transfer payment was further intensified. In 2005, almost half (specifically, 47.3%) of the standard gap between locally obtained revenues and expenditures was subsidized with the ordinary transfer payment of the central government.

Others under the general transfer payment are granted for relatively specific purposes. For example, transfer payment for areas inhabited by ethnic minorities and those as a reward/subsidy for relevant counties/townships support the local finance of particular regions. Regulatory wage transfer payment is essentially a fiscal measure aimed at increasing the salary of the staff working with administrative institutions whereby such increases, in prosperous regions, shall be borne by the local government, otherwise (partially) covered by the central government, as the case may be. With an even more clear-cut purpose, the transfer payment for the tax reform was introduced to cover the local fiscal gap at the township and/or village level caused by the tax reform started in 2002.

In short, transfer payments other than the general transfer payment are all based on explicit purposes despite the fact that they have been granted as fiscal subsidy for local governments in nature. As such subsidy should be used as per the stipulation by the central government, these are actually quasi-special transfer payments.

Special transfer payment is another major component of China's transfer payment system, much larger in amount than the general transfer payment.

The local financial gap that resulted from centralization under the tax-sharing system has been considered the major cause of the financial difficulties at the grass-roots level. According to the opinions of academic circle, this situation was characterized by centralized authority in contrast with decentralized duties and responsibilities. Although the tax-sharing system only provided the sharing of revenues between the central governments and the provincial governments, the effects of revenue centralization had wide-ranging effect as the revenue sharing below the provincial level should be determined by the provincial government, which would be definitely accompanied by the centralization of fiscal powers. There was a popular saying that "the central government saw its windfall, the provincial government managed limpingly, the county government had to resort to a makeshift solution, while the township government could do nothing but cry" after the introduction of the tax-sharing system, a real picture of that time. Obviously, as their financial resources were taken by the central government, local governments, especially the governments at the county and township levels, fell in dismay, which have been considered a major reason behind the increasingly heavy burden borne by farmers in the Midwest after the mid-1990s.

However, from the perspective of the transfer payment system, we can see something has been omitted: the part taken by the central government actually was not spent, but returned to local governments by means of transfer payment. It would be obviously unfair if we base our research solely on the total amount and pin the local financial difficulties on the tax-sharing system. The following is an analysis of the impact of the tax-sharing system on the financial status at the county/township level based on the corresponding financial data, with an emphasis on transfer payment.

The effects of revenue centralization under this system has been transmitted downward, as accompanied by the centralization of authority, which can be most easily seen from the financial situations at the county/township level. Now we will make a comparison of the conditions of county-level finance before and after the introduction of the tax-sharing system. In 1994 when the system was already in force, the central government collected CNY 107.22 billion of VAT and consumption duty from the county/township level; however, if we calculate the sum according to the previous fiscal system, the revenues at the county/township level would be approximately CNY 200 billion (centrally controlled revenues of county/township governments + revenues locally retained by county/township governments). Thus, it can be roughly grasped that 50% of the revenues at these two levels were centralized under the tax-sharing system.

The expenditures at the county and township levels in the pre-reform 1993 and post-reform 1994 amounted to CNY 145.9 billion and 170.3 billion respectively, showing a considerable year-on-year rise, instead of cut-down of local expenditures. Comparing the revenues and expenditures before and after the implementation of this system, we will know that the pre-reform and post-reform deficits were CNY 8.64 billion and 73.59 billion, respectively. According to the data of 1994, the latter accounted for around 37% of the total revenues at the county and township levels (including both local revenues and turnover to the central government). This was the microcosm of the general fiscal situation, indicating that the relationship between the central government and provincial governments was completely copied by the county and township levels.

However, transfer payment is not considered hereinbefore. In fact, the central government has granted substantial subsidies, including tax rebates, special transfer payment, transitional transfer payment, institutional subsidy, etc., in the form of transfer payments since the implementation of the tax-sharing system in order to make up local deficits. In 1994, the central government granted CNY 238.64 billion in the form of transfer payment to local governments (at/below the provincial level). In 2002, the amount increased fourfold to CNY 735.18 billion. The annual average growth rate during this period was 15%. So, have these subsidies been delivered to the county and township levels, like the effects of revenue centralization, to offset the deficits resulting from the reform?

The institutional quota subsidy is equivalent to financial transfer payment as mentioned earlier. It is comprised of miscellaneous subsidies granted to the county government by the government of a higher level in the form of transfer payment under the applicable fiscal system. As shown in the table above, the subsidies granted by the government of a higher level to the county/township level in the form of transfer payment witnessed a substantial increase after the introduction of the tax-sharing system, which mainly included a tax rebate increment of CNY 58.03 billion. The net subsidy for the first year of the reform reached CNY 65.06 billion, compared with almost nil before the reform, indicating the pre-reform deficit (CNY 73.5 billion) was basically maintained. Thus, although the tax-sharing-system-based reform brought on the centralization of financial resources at the county and township levels, which resulted in increased deficits, such outgo was basically made up by transfer payments, and thus the pre-reform balance was maintained (Table 3.2).

This was the situation immediately after the tax-sharing system came into force. As the rate of tax rebates was designed in favor of the central government, the determination of 1:0.3 for VAT increment would result in a sharp decrease in the proportion of tax rebates. It is justifiable to believe that with the passage of time, more and more revenues would be under the control of the central government, and local deficits would also increase. Then, what effects would the tax-sharing system produce in the long run? Would the turnover to the central government from locally tax revenues increase?

The analysis of the variation in the centrally controlled proportion of revenues obtained at the county/township level should be based on the net value of centrally controlled VAT and consumption duty by subtracting tax rebates from centrally controlled revenues and then adding the subtracted part to the revenues obtained at the county/township level. On the whole, the centrally controlled proportion of revenues obtained at the county/township level has been continuously increasing. It was only slightly more than 10% in 1995. By 2002, it had increased to nearly 30%.

The centralization of revenues under the tax-sharing system would inevitably lead to ever-increasing local deficits. As we have made a comparison between the fiscal condition before and immediately after the introduction of the tax-sharing system, we will provide a survey of the situation after it has been implemented for nearly ten years. First of all, deficits at the county/township level have been increasing, especially since 1998. it increased from CNY 70 billion in 1994 to CNY 100 billion in 1998, and finally to approximately CNY 300 billion in 2002. However, statistics show that more and more subsidies have been granted in an

Table 3.2 Transfer payment, turnover and net subsidy for governments of the county/township level before and after the introduction of the tax-sharing system (*unit* CNY 1 billion)

Item	1993	1994
Tax rebates		58.03
Special transfer payment	27.66	29.91
Institutional quota subsidy	6.73	8.17
Total subsidy	34.39	96.11
Institutional turnover	−25.54	−24.67
Special turnover	−8.64	−6.38
Total turnover	−34.18	−31.05
Net subsidy	0.21	65.06

attempt to make up such deficits. Now the net deficit (after a subsidy is granted by the government of a higher level) at the county/township level can be calculated by aid of the formula below:

$$\text{Gross deficit} = \text{local revenues} - \text{local expenditures}$$

$$\text{Net deficit} = \text{local revenues} - \text{local expenditures} + \text{net revenue of the subsidy granted by the government at a higher level}$$

The role of subsidies granted by the government of a higher level zooms in when we compare the gross and net deficits as shown in Table 3.3. Due to the revenues centralization caused by the tax-sharing system, the gross deficit at the county/township level has been ever increasing from CNY 73.6 billion in 1994 to CNY 308.8 billion in 2002. However, the net deficit has remained steady at CNY 5–15 billion thanks to the synchronous adding of net subsidy by the government of a higher level.

The aggregate analysis on the impacts of the tax-sharing system above shows that the increased deficit arising from the centralization of revenues obtained at the county/township level has been made up by transfer payments. Thus, from this perspective, the tax-sharing system should not be held responsible for the financial difficulties of county/township governments. However, this is just an aggregate analysis. If the regional imbalance was not eliminated by the distribution of transfer payments, certain county/township governments would inevitably face financial difficulties. What follows is an analysis of the role played by transfer payments in narrowing inter-regional financial differences.

Transfer payment can meet two ends: (a) achieving inter-regional fiscal equalization so that the residents of different regions are entitled to similar public services; and (b) enabling the central government to impose constraints on local governments' behaviors. It is worth noting that such redistribution of fiscal revenues differs from the remuneration distribution under the modern enterprise system. The latter follows the principle of efficiency, obeying the rule of "To each according to his contribution", while the former gives priority to equalization over efficiency. Now let's see if the expected equalization has been achieved under the tax-sharing system.

Table 3.3 Deficits at the county/township level (*unit* CNY 1 billion)

Year	1993	1994	1995	1996	1997	1998	1999	2000	2001	2002
Revenue	137.2	96.7	126.1	157.8	149.7	167.7	242.6	263.6	309.6	322.5
Expenditure	145.8	170.3	204.2	245.1	239.0	265.1	373.4	419.9	525.3	631.3
Gross deficit	−8.6	−73.6	−78.1	−87.3	−89.3	−97.4	−130.8	−156.3	−215.7	−308.8
Net subsidy	0.2	65.1	66.5	74.1	78.9	83.7	109.8	145.1	210.8	297.9
Net deficit	−8.4	−8.5	−11.6	−13.2	−10.4	−13.7	−21.0	−11.2	−4.9	−10.9

As China clings to balanced budget and allows no budget deficits, such is the case of most regions—

$$\text{Budget Outlays} = \text{Budgeted Revenue of the Corresponding Level} + \text{Net Subsidy}$$

Now let's first examine the variation in per capita budgetary income since the adoption of the tax-sharing system in three major regions, namely East China, Central China and West China. Statistics show that since the adoption of the tax-sharing system, Central China and West China have witnessed slow increases in their fiscal revenues at the county/township level at an almost identical rate. For instance, in 2003, per capita budgeted revenue in Central China and West China were CNY 212 and 210 respectively. However, the per capita budgeted revenue at the county/township level in East China rose more than four-fold within a decade, from CNY 113 in 1994 to CNY 485 in 2003 as a result of rapid industrialization. Correspondingly, the revenue gap between East China and Central/West China rose from around CNY 35 to CNY 270 during this period.

As for the per capita expenditure, it approximates per capita income plus per capita subsidy. Statistics show that inter-regional differences in per capita expenditure have been smaller than those in per capita income. In 2003, the per capita expenditure in East China was CNY 750, while that of the Central China and West China were CNY 500 and 571 respectively. Thus the difference between the highest revenue of East China and the lowest revenue of Central China was CNY 250, 20 less than that in per capita income. This was a result of inter-regional transfer payments. However, it is obvious that the inter-regional difference of per capita expenditure has augmented steadily in spite of the ever-increasing inter-regional transfer payments. Less than CNY 50 in 1994, the difference of per capita expenditure among these three regions increased to CNY 250 in 2003, indicating that transfer payments were far from enough for eliminating the inequality arising from unbalanced regional development.

An analysis based on the comparison of statistical data of many years shows that the per capita income in Central China was basically equal to that in West China, but there were obvious differences in per capita expenditure between them, which was mainly caused by the fact more transfer payments have been injected into West China. Densely populated as it is, the mostly agricultural Central China has been burdened with substantial expenditures on rural public services and a large population in financial supply at the county/township level, but has received the least transfer payment by the central government. Due to such deficits, the county/township governments in this region naturally resorted to various means to increase extra-budgetary revenues, resulting in the ever-increasing burden plaguing farmers as well as social tensions.

So, what was the problem with the distribution of transfer payments? And why did it fail to achieve an obvious equalization?

The transfer payments granted by the central government can be divided into three categories, namely, VAT and consumption tax rebates, special subsidies and miscellaneous subsidies. The first category is related to the tax-sharing system, as described hereinabove. The second includes some temporary special financial subsidies that are small in amount and diverse in assortment (up to 100 to more than 200 items were granted within a year), as granted by the higher level. Before 2000, the third category mainly included some institutional subsidies in small amount, established with the view of partially maintaining the relationship between the central government and local governments in terms of subsidy and turnover. Since then, the central government has granted a large amount of various transfer payments in its pursuit of inter-regional equalization, such as the general transfer payment, transfer payment for the tax reform, regulatory wage transfer payment, and tax rebates from the income tax base established in 2002. These are all simply classified as miscellaneous subsidies, for this issue is not our focus.

Among the three categories of transfer payments, tax rebates have witnessed an ever-decreasing proportion, which is in relation to the design of the tax-sharing system. As various subsidies have been granted by the central government in the form of transfer payments since 2000, the proportion of special subsidies has also dropped rapidly. In 1994 tax rebates and special subsidies accounted for more than 90% of the total amount of transfer payments. Ten years later (or in 2003), their proportions decreased from 61 and 31% to about 18 and 23% respectively, while the proportion of miscellaneous subsidies increased to 59%. The miscellaneous subsidies mainly included regulatory wage subsidy with a view to helping maintain normal local daily financial operations (16%), transfer payment for the tax reform (7.9%), and the general transfer payment aimed at an inter-regional balance of financial resources (7.3%). That is to say, most of the miscellaneous subsidies were aimed at balancing financial resources which, theoretically speaking, favored central and western regions. And it seems that along with the structural transformation of the entire system of transfer payments, more and more transfer payments have flowed to these regions.

However, a region-by-region examination reveals that reality was quite different from what we supported. The annual variations in these three categories of transfer payments in different regions are illustrated by the following three figures (Figs. 3.2, 3.3, and 3.4), where data are all per capita ones.

Interestingly, the three categories of subsidies granted to central regions have been always the lowest, with the other two regions playing "Box and Cox" regarding subsidies. Tax rebates granted to the eastern region far exceeded those to central and western regions, while the western region has obtained the most special and miscellaneous subsidies. What's surprising is that as far as special and miscellaneous subsidies are concerned, the central regions were less favored than the eastern regions. In 2003, the per capita tax rebates, special subsidy per capita, and miscellaneous subsidy per capita obtained by the central regions were CNY 44, 75, and 194 respectively, all less than those granted to the eastern (CNY 97, 81, and 199 respectively) and western (CNY 45, 96 and 250 respectively) regions, perfectly manifesting its disadvantages in terms of per capita fiscal expenditures.

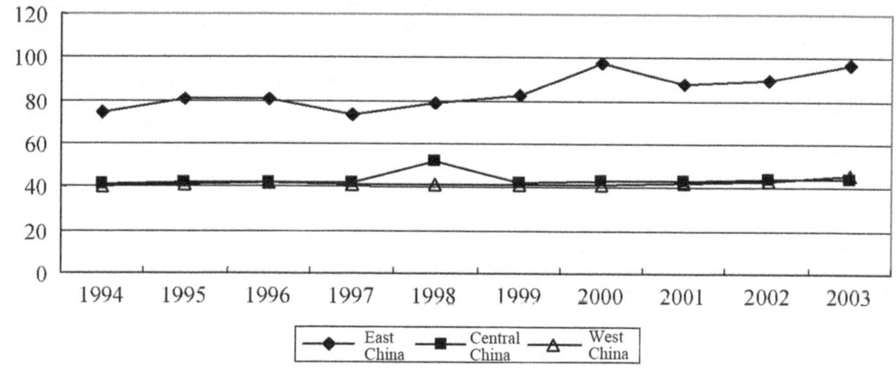

Fig. 3.2 Per capita tax rebates at the county/township level in eastern, central and western regions of China (*unit* CNY)

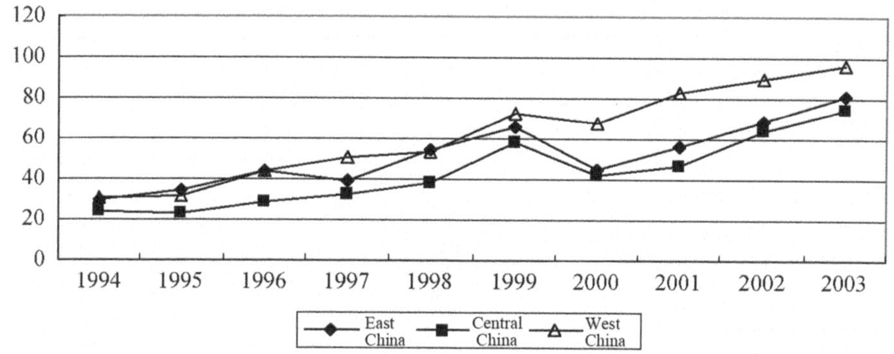

Fig. 3.3 Special subsidy per capita at the county/township level in eastern, central and western regions of China (*unit*: CNY)

To summarize, the tax-sharing system has enabled the central government to grant tax rebates and transfer payments to local governments to make up local deficits with the centralized local revenues that increased the proportion of centrally controlled revenues. From the perspective of the national situation, it has been basically successful. However, after examining the financial condition of each region, we found a serious inter-regional imbalance, which has undoubtedly deviated from the original intention of this system. In the decade since its implementation, the two proportions (viz. proportion of fiscal revenues to the GDP and the centrally controlled proportion of fiscal revenues) and state capacity have been

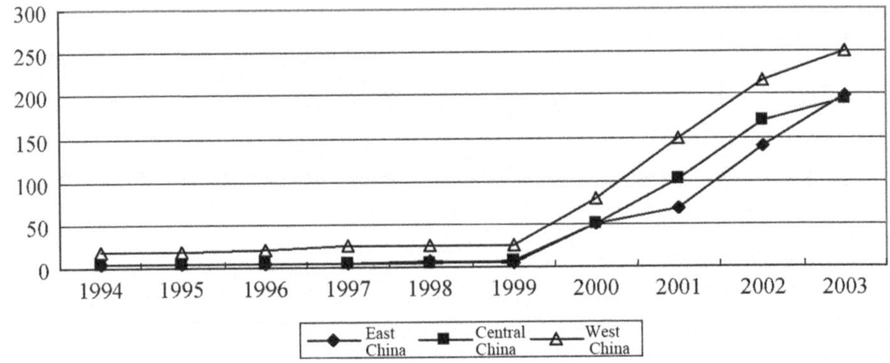

Fig. 3.4 Miscellaneous subsidy per capita at the county/township level in eastern, central and western regions of China (*unit* CNY)

basically enhanced, but the imbalance of financial resources and public services arising from uneven regional development was further aggravated, for the central regions have lagged even farther behind the other two regions.

The foregoing study only included the direct effects of the tax-sharing system. It should be noted that its indirect effects still remain to be examined. According to our empirical phenomena, the actual inter-regional difference among the eastern, cental and western regions has far exceeded what transfer payments could make up, despite the uneven allocation of transfer payments. Regardless of the ever-decreasing proportion of tax rebates granted to the eastern region and the ever-increasing proportion of transfer payments received by the other two regions, there has been a far cry from regional equalization in terms of public services, which could be hardly explained by the distribution of transfer payments. As noted in the literature review, the discussion on the distribution of revenues, expenditures and transfer payments only covers the financial aspect, so we need to delve into governmental behaviors on the political side in order to truly and completely understand the factors influencing revenues distribution. As a profound reform, the implementation of tax-sharing system has not only brought about centralized fiscal revenues and intensified transfer payments, but also influenced the government-enterprise relationship and the extra-budgetary revenues of local governments, which reshaped the behaviour paradigm of local governments to a great extent in the past decade.

The implementation of tax-sharing system has been the most significant reform of the fiscal system ever since the reform and opening up, whereby the central government has enhanced the aforesaid two proportions, strengthened its control over economic development adjustment as well as revenue distribution, and established a standard for its relationship with local governments, extricating itself from the plight of never-ending negotiations regarding redistribution with local governments. Meanwhile, it also has significant and far-reaching impacts on the relationships between the central government and local governments, the relationship between governments and enterprises as well as the inter-regional connection, which have been revealed gradually in the decade following the adoption of the system.

Chapter 4
Land Fiscal Revenues

From the perspective of the relationship between the central government and local governments, whether the tax-sharing system is a centralizing or decentralizing reform has given rise to much controversy. From the stand-point of revenues distribution, it is undoubtedly a centralizing reform, for 75% of the VAT increments of local governments have been centralized, and the centrally/locally controlled proportions of fiscal revenues have witnessed subversive changes, which is a perfect manifestation of the centralization of fiscal revenues. However, fiscal expenditures of both the central government and local governments have not been decreased as expected under the tax-sharing system, instead, they kept rising all along. This has become the major issues for debates from the stand-point of both revenues and expenditures. As such a system effectuated revenues centralization without modifying the expenditures pattern of the central government and local governments, transfer payments should be granted to local governments so as to cover their expenditures, which has been proved hereinabove. It should be noted that in such a way, the share of fiscal revenues that is to be controlled autonomously by the local governments was greatly reduced, but their expenditure burden has not been relieved. What's more, the burden has kepting increasing, mirroring the situation of "centralized authority in contrast with decentralized duties and responsibilities" as described by the academic circle.

Under the pressure produced by such a system, local governments began to seek new means to increase local revenue growth. As an interest subject in its pursuit of fiscal revenue growth under the fiscal responsibility system, local governments further enhanced, instead of taking the edge off their subjective consciousness under a heavy expenditure constraint after the implementation of the tax-sharing system. To obtain new discretionary fiscal revenues to relieve their expenditure pressure is an urgent issue confronting local governments.

In view of the shortage of urban construction land arising form the influx of foreign investment, mass migration of labor from central and western regions, as well as the industrialization and urbanization in coastal areas, which have been typical of the 21st century, the reform of the urban land system and the farmland

F. Zhou and M. Tan, *Relationship between the Central Government and Local Governments of Contemporary China*, Social Development Experiences in China,
DOI 10.1007/978-981-10-4388-8_4

expropriation system has provided a guarantee to meet the economic and institutional demands in their large-scale land requisition, development and transfer activities.

4.1 Land Requisition and Land Revenues of Governments

There are two types of land ownership in China, namely, ownership by the whole people and collective ownership. Under the former is state-owned land, and all land in the cities is owned by the State. According to the *Amendment to the Constitution of the People's Republic of China* of 1982 that "land in the cities is owned by the State" (Article 10), while lands of collective ownership belong to the rural collective.

Land requisition is a measure of nationalizing the collectively-owned rural lands in accordance with legal conditions and procedures. In the process of urbanization, urban construction is only allowed on state-owned lands (rather than collectively-owned lands), which herein shall include both "the state-owned land and the land, which was originally under collective ownership by farmers, has been requisitioned by the State" (Article 43), indicating that if urban construction necessarily involves collective-owned land, the collective ownership shall be transformed by means of expropriation. It can be sold, appropriated, leased or transferred only after its collective ownership is transformed into an ownership of the State. The transformation is defined as land requisition. It is usually completed by local governments.

The Land Administration Law of the People's Republic of China is the legal basis for transforming agricultural land into non-agricultural construction land. According to the *Land Administration Law of the People's Republic of China* of 1998, "the State may, in the public interest and by operation of law, expropriate or requisition land for its use." (Article 2) As the right of requisitioning lands is monopolized by the State, land requisition falls within governmental administrative behaviors. More specifically, local governments exercise their powers over land requisition and monopolize land resources within a specific territorial scope on behalf of the State. In such a way, land requisition, as a policy made to the law, has become a major approach to possessing/obtaining rural resources with mandatory force of the state.

Land requisition shall entail due compensation to the original owner (collective) and users (farmers) based on the "the original purposes of the land expropriated". For example, compensation for the expropriation of arable land generally includes: (a) land compensation, which amounts to 6–10 times of the annual average agriculture production value of the previous 3 years; (b) resettlement compensation, calculated as per agricultural population to be resettled ×4–6 times of the annual average agriculture production value of the previous 3 years (Note that the agricultural population to be resettled = area of arable land as expropriated/previous arable land per capita of the region expropriated); and (c) compensation for attachments and green crops on the land, as determined by local governments.

After the government transforms collective-owned agricultural land into state-owned land via requisition, any organization and/or individual may apply for the use of state-owned land in accordance with law (Article 43), which is the most important means of obtaining the lands necessary for China's urbanization. The right to sell state-owned land is monopolized by the state, so "no organization or individual is permitted to appropriate, buy, sell or engage in the transfer of land by other unlawful means" (Article 2).

The land-use right could not be obtained for free. As the user of the state-owned land, a construction unit shall pay "land use right transfer fees" to the government. During the process, "the state implements the system of paid-for use for state-owned land in accordance with law" (Article 2). The use of state-owned land for a construction project shall be obtained in the form of "paid-for use", except that for non-profit undertakings may be obtained in the form of appropriation. "A construction unit that has obtained the use right of state-owned land in the form of paid-for use… may use the land only upon the payment of fees for paid-for land use and other fees…" (Article 55).

In discussing a government's land revenues, we usually consider the land use right transfer fees while ignoring other revenues. Now let's see what "a government's land revenues" means. It refers to the revenues obtained from taxation, fee-collecting or managing business, land requisition and land transfer. It includes not only the land use right transfer fees, but also various land-related tax revenues. Strictly speaking, land use right transfer fees are essentially the "package" rent paid by a land user for using the land for an allotted period, which falls within quasi-business revenues obtained from land development and transfer, and thus shall be excluded from the fiscal revenues of the government. Regarding tax revenues, there are rarely major taxes items or fees imposed on land requisition and transfer under the current tax system. Land-related revenues of the government are included in the various taxes and fees which have been excluded in systematic statistics. Therefore, we need to "winnow" such revenues from taxes paid to the government during the analysis process. In view of the limited available information, this book only attempts to make its analysis roughly accurate. In contrast with the various items and huge inter-regional differences in taxation, the land use right transfer fees has been uniformly collected in quite considerable amounts, so we will discussed them separately.

Land-related tax revenues of local governments can be divided into the following four categories:

1. Tax directly related to land. It includes the city and town land use tax, land value increment tax, both of which are levied by the land tax system. It also includes tax on land occupation, and deed tax, both of which are levied by the financial system.

According to the *Provisional Regulations on Use tax of land in Cities and Towns of the People's Republic of China* issued by the State Council in 1988, the use tax of land shall be calculated as per the actual area (rather than value) of land occupied by the taxpayer at the following designated rates: major cities: CNY 0.5–10 per square meter; medium-sized cities: CNY 0.4–8 per square meter; small-sized cities: CNY 0.3–6 per square meter; counties, organic towns, and industrial and mining areas: CNY 0.2–4 per square meter. Thus, the use tax of land cannot reflect the added value and differential rent of land which, coupled with the absolute limits of tax set by the aforesaidregulations, has quite deviated from the actual situation.

Levying the land value increment tax is one of the tax adjustment measures aimed at standardizing the order of land and real estate transactions and adjusting land increment revenues. China promulgated *Provisional Regulations on Increment Tax on Land Value of the People's Republic of China* (hereinafter referred to as the "*Regulations*") in 1994, which was then supplemented by *Implementing Rules of Provisional Regulations on Increment Tax on Land Value of the People's Republic of China* specifying the means of levying increment tax on land value. The major purpose of the increment tax on land value is to keep the order of the real estate development market and curb the behaviors of reaping staggering profits in developing and transfering real estate. Therefore, it mainly affects real estate developement enterprises (especially the developers of villas, apartments, office buildings and other high-end projects) and individual speculations concerning buildings under construction. It is provided under the *Regulations* that increment tax on land value shall be exempted if taxpayers are constructing ordinary standard residences for sale, where the amount of added value does not exceed 20% of the sum of deduction items (viz. development costs plus taxes). Thus, any individual who buys ordinary standard dwelling house for their own use will not be affected by the increment tax on land value. For high-end building properties, the aforesaid increment tax on land value shall be paid at a definite rate by developers for their profit magins (viz. amount of increment) usually exceed the stipulated initial sum for increment tax on land value, which will result in a decrease in the income from primary land development.

Compared with the tax on using urban land, the increment tax on land value may reflect the differential rent of land and incremental benefits to a certain degree. In recent years, the increment tax on land value has become a major component of the direct taxes on land.

The farmland occupation tax shall be paid by any unit or individual engaged in house-building on farmland or other non-agricultural construction to the state as per the occupied area. According to the *Interim Regulations of the People'Republic of China on Farmland Occupation Tax* of 1987, the farmland occupation tax shall be levied in lump sum as per the actual as per the stipulated rate based on the area of farmland occupied by the taxpayers. Such farmland may be owned by either the state or the rural collective. Rural residents building houses on farmland may be allowed a 50% reduction of the standard amount of the farmland occupation tax. For special economic zones, economic and technological development zones and those developed areas with particularly limited farmland per capita, the applicable tax amount may be increased appropriately, but shall not exceed 50% of the standard amount. In view of its similarity to the use tax on land, the farmland occupation tax is also levied as per the area (rather than value) of the occupied land in lump sum, so it cannot fully reveal the added value of the land. Levied in lump sum as it is, the farmland occupation tax can indirectly reflect the variations in the area of requisitioned or transferred land. In 2002, the farmland occupation tax levied in such a background in Zhejiang Province amounted to CNY 1.23 billion, accounting for 2.17% of the fiscal revenues of the province. The farmland occupation tax of Shaoxing County of this province reached CNY 77.39 million in Shaoxing County in 2003, accounting for 5.7% of the local fiscal revenues of the year.

The deed tax is one of the property taxes imposed on real estate subject to ownership transfer that should be paid by the property right bearer. The applicable law is the *Provisional Regulations on Title Deed Tax of the People's Republic of China* re-promulgated on July 7, 1997. The deed tax has been levied mainly on land and real estate since October 1, 1997. From the perspective of tax base and rates, the deed tax can better reflect the differential earnings from land, compared with other taxes on land. It is also the most substantive item of direct taxation on land. In 2002, the deed tax collected in Zhejiang Province amounted to CNY 3.016 billion, accounting for 5.32% of the fiscal revenues of the province that year. It reached CNY 110.27 million in Shaoxing County in 2003, accounting for 8.2 of the local fiscal revenues of the year.

In Zhejiang Province, the total direct taxes on land accounted for 3.1% of the total fiscal revenues (including the centrally controlled fiscal revenues) or 6.3% of local fiscal revenues; and in Shaoxing County of this province, these two proportions were around 6.2 and 14% respectively. It is worth mentioning that under the tax-sharing system, all these land revenues belong to local governments. Although the total sum of land tax is not much, the tax is very important for local fiscal revenue, for the additional part of the tax, no matter how trifling is the sum, all belongs to the local finance.

From the stand-point of the internal structure, each of the four types of taxes plays an important but different role. Levied based on the area of land as per a fixed rate, the use tax on land and farmland occupation tax can hardly reflect the added value of the land, which is a manifestation of its poor "growth", but may adequately reflect the variations of the area of land requisitioned by local governments. On the contrary, increment tax on land value and deed tax may reveal the changes of the value of land, but the former has not been levied yet. So, of these four types of taxes, deed tax is the largest in volume, highest in growth and most important for local governments.

2. Although the direct taxes on land are minor in proportion (5–15%) to local fiscal revenues, the contribution of land operation to local fiscal revenues is not limited to such direct taxes. Land revenues shall also include some indirect taxes in relation to land requisition and transfer.

Considering that no consensus has been reached on the definition of indirect tax on land in a strict sense, it is herein interpreted as the taxes arising from the industries (mainly including construction and real estate) directly driven by land requisition and transfer. Of course, some of the revenues from construction and real estate have no relation to land requisition and transfer, and the tertiary industry and others are just the opposite, resulting in a blurred boundary between them. Therefore, here we are only aimed at a rough estimation of the indirect taxes on land with a view to evaluate the indirect benefits of local governments arising from land requisition and transfer.

These indirect taxes mainly include:

(1) Business tax in relation to land transfer, with the business tax paid by local government-run land developers included. In 2003, the business tax levied on revenues from land transfer in Zhejiang Province reached around CNY 1.1 billion, accounting for about 2% of the local fiscal revenues.
(2) Business tax and corporate income tax on constructors and real estate developers. As the performance of construction business and the real estate industry is closely related to urban land development and transfer, the size of business tax may directly mirror the contribution of land development to local fiscal revenues. In 2003, the business tax on constructors and real estate developers reached CNY 0.23 billion (CNY 0.14 billion and 0.09 billion, respectively) in Shaoxing County, accounting for 17% of the local fiscal revenues. On the other side, the corporate income tax from these two industries (tax payable to local governments inclusive) amounted to CNY 0.038 billion, accounting for 2.8% of the local fiscal revenues.
(3) Real estate and urban real estate tax. In 2003, urban real estate tax amounted to CNY 0.061 billion, accounting for 4.5% of the local fiscal revenues.

The sum of the three items above roughly accounted for 26% of local fiscal revenues. Note that these do not cover all indirect taxes arising from land development obtained by all the governments. The data above are based on a conservative estimation.

Indirect taxes are usually ignored in research. It is found out that in sharp contrast with direct taxes on land, indirect taxes on land are considerable in proportion to revenues, which means that land development has indirectly promoted the growth of local fiscal revenues.

As the majority of direct and indirect taxes on land are paid to local governments instead of the central government, the direct and indirect taxes arising from land development mostly fall within local fiscal revenues (the central government is entitled to a share of 60% of the corporate income tax. In 2003, the corporate income tax on constructors and real estate developers in Shaoxing County paid to the central government amounted to CNY 0.057 billion, accounting for only 3.3% of its turnover of the year). From the perspective of local governments, it is "securer" to financially rely on indirect taxes than on direct taxes, because it is highly possible for direct taxes to be classified as payable to the central government should their growth be too fast, according to the pattern of the fiscal reform in recent years.

As a major component of the fiscal revenues, land revenues can hardly be accurately "segregated" in statistics and management, which is a result of the fact that the former tax system cannot adapt to changes in the structure of local economy. Under the current tax system, the diverse and deregulated taxation on land, coupled with the fact that direct revenues from land principally rely on lump-sum taxation while indirect revenues are mainly sourced from the construction industry, will certainly encourage local governments to expand land requisition-based construction business while ignoring the economic development and sustainable growth of tax sources.

3. Charges by government departments. The charges include those in direct relation to land, such as cultivated land reclamation fees and paid utilization charges on newly added construction land (charged by competent land administration departments) as well as various other items charged during land requisition/transfer and real estate development.

These charges on land can be divided into the following three categories as per the competent departments that receive them:

(1) Charges by land administration departments. A survey indicates that the charges by land administration departments in Shaoxing County in 2003 mainly included regulated fees (CNY 60.11 million), special charges (CNY 106.45 million) and fees for the paid use of land newly added for construction (CNY 31.1 million), accounting for approx. 10% of the total land price. The regulated fees mainly included farmland reclamation fees (CNY 12.59 million), administrative expenses (CNY 9.13 million), and operational expenditures (CNY 38.49 million); and special charges mainly included publicizing fee (CNY 0.18 million), compensation for house demolition (CNY 30.19 million), conversion target charges (CNY 53.5 million) and compensation for the re-take of state-owned land (CNY 22.58 million).
(2) Charges by financial departments. The charges mainly included the land use right transfer fees, which will be discussed separately. In addition, land royalty and rents are collected in many regions, subject to the respective regulations of the local governments (or local laws and regulations).
(3) Charges by other departments. The process from land requisition to transfer inevitably entails charges by the authorities of various sectors such as agriculture, real estate, irrigation works, transportation, post and telecommunications, cultural relic, civil air defense, forestry, etc., subject to the standards compiled independently by the respective provincial governments.

An estimate of the total land charges is unfeasible, for items (2) and (3) as described above have not been clearly defined. However, charges by land administration departments reached nearly CNY 0.2 billion, so the total land charges will of course far exceed the direct taxes on land (CNY 0.18 billion), not to mention the other two items. It can be seen that greater emphasis has been put on such charges, rather than taxes. Based on a rough estimation of the situation in Shaoxing County, the direct tax on land, indirect tax on land and the aforesaid charges were in proportion of around 1:2:1.5, with the land use right transfer fees excluded.

4. The land use right transfer fees are not taxes, but rents arising from the lands leased by the government.

Such rent shall be paid by the land user in lump sum as advance payment. For convenience, the land use right transfer fees herein are referred to as the gross earnings from land transfer (calculated as per transaction value), and the net income from land use right transfer fees equals the land use right transfer fees minus the cost of land transfer. So, the total land use right transfer fees of the state shall amount to the total revenues payable to local governments arising from land transfer in the form of auction, agreement, etc. According to a report, China's gross land use right transfer fees from 1992 to 2003 went up to more than CNY 1000 billion, of which the overwhelming majority (more specifically, more than CNY 910 billion) was obtained from 2001 to 2003, and the net income from such fund accounted for around 1/4. A report by China Index Academy (CIA) reveals that the gross land use right transfer fees reached CNY 1.5 trillion in 2009, and major cities constituted the key growth point, considering 70 cities across the country witnessed a year-on-year growth rate of more than 100% in the land use right transfer fees, with Shanghai (CNY 8.21 billion, which is the highest), Beijing, Hangzhou ranking the top three and the top 20 cities claiming a share of up to CNY 621 billion, with a year-on-year increase rate of 108%. According to Xu Shaoshi, Minister of Land and Resources, the land use right transfer fees of 2010 totaled CNY 2.7 trillion, nearly 100% higher than at of 2009.

Costs of land transfer consist of:

(1) Taxes on land transfer, which are actually included in the above-mentioned taxes, except for land-based charges and funds payable to the government, such as the International Fund for Agricultural Development (IFAD) and social security fund;
(2) Land compensation fees, including compensation for land, resettlement, green crops, demolition of ground attachments, etc. to farmers and the village collective, which will be discussed in Sect. 4.3;
(3) Land development fees, which refer to the average development costs of passage, water supply (and sewage line), electricity, and communication outside the red line of parcels and those of land leveling within the parcel at each land level, depending on the regional economic development; and
(4) Operating expenditure arising from land transfer payable to competent land administration departments, which equals 2–5% of the balance of the land use right transfer fees, with taxes involved in land tranfer excluded.

A rough estimate of the costs of and income from the land use right transfer fees may be obtained based on our survey of the fiscal situation in Zhejiang Province: in each of the three regions surveyed by us, the land use right transfer fees uniformly totaled approximately CNY 2 billion in 2003, of which the net income accounted for 15–30%. Thus, it is appropriate to assume a net income ratio of 20% for other regions in Zhejiang Province. This is undoubtedly a huge sum of revenues for local governments.

To sum up, land revenues of the government are characterized by the following:

Firstly, the land revenues are huge in volume. The total land revenues of a government may be obtained by summing up the four components, namely, direct taxes, indirect taxes, charges and net income from the land use right transfer fees. According to our rough estimate of the fiscal situation of Shaoxing County in 2003, land revenues summed up to nearly CNY 1.4 billion, equivalent to the fiscal revenues of the local government of the year. The other two regions were about the same. These are calculated based on the net income from land use right transfer fees. If based on the total amount of the land use right transfer fees, land revenues went up to CNY 2.7 billion, doubling the local fiscal revenues. From the foregoing analysis of the four components of land revenues, it can be roughly estimated that direct taxes, indirect taxes, charges by competent departments and the land use right transfer fees are in proportion of 1:2:1.5:2.5, or more accurately, their proportions to the total land revenues of a government are 14, 29, 21, and 36% respectively. It is worth noting that this estimate is based on the situation of the three regions in Zhejiang Province. There might be huge differences elsewhere.

Secondly, the various tax items can hardly reflect the differential incomes. On the whole, land revenues are principally characterized by their numerous items and poor management. There are only four items falling within direct taxes on land, of which two items are levied based on the area of land and one item is basically suspended, which can hardly reflect the differential incomes from land. Indirect taxes are mainly comprised of the business tax on construction and real estate projects that are driven by investment and construction expansion, rather than the sustainable local economic development. As many as the hairs of an ox, these charges can be hardly enumerated.

Finally, as most of the items are provided under local regulations, land revenues are subject to poor management. To a certain extent, Local governments are free to impose land-related taxes, as almost all the land revenues may be retained by them. Charges by relevant departments are usually governed by local governments, while the authority over cost accounting of the land use right transfer fees are also decentralized, resulting in an extremely low transparency. The land revenues have increased rapidly and thus become the major source of local fiscal revenues in the eastern region, but the improvement of the supervision over the management and use of land taxes and charges lags behind.

4.2 Land Revenues

Generally considered as very significant for the local finance, land revenues have cultivated another governmental fiscal system, the second finance, in addition to the budgetary revenues finance of local governments. The second finance under the sole control of local governments involves substantial capital and centers on land revenues, therefore also known as "land finance". Sayings popular among local governments, "the primary finance relies on industrialization, while the secondary finances depend on land" and "Bread comes from the first finance, while construction depends on the second finance", illustrate the sources of incomes and items of expenditures under the dualistic financial pattern. This is a concise but express interpretation of the significance of land finance to local governments. Our survey indicates that this view is only partly correct, because besides the secondary finance, the primary finance is becoming more and more dependent on land, rather than industry. The following sections will explain the basic characteristics of land finance based on case studies of the situation in Chang'an District of Xi'an City, Shaanxi Province and Shaoxing County, Zhejiang Province.

1. Relationship Between Revenues Structure and Land Development in Chang'an District of Xi'an City, Shaanxi Province.

Chang'an County was established in the Western Han Dynasty (202BC-AD8) and made the capital in several dynasties. Located only 8.7 km away from the downtown area of Xi'an City, it became a newly-added district with Weiqu and Guodu, two development zones dominated by science and technology enterprises and universities, of the city in September, 2002. The former county system was repealed at the same time. Since the beginning of the 21st century, it has been chosen to be the site of the college town in Xi'an, witnessing large-scale land development.

The revenues of a local government are generally composed of three parts, namely budgeted revenues, revenues from financial funds and extra budgeted revenues. From 1999 to 2003, great changes characterized by the gradually increase of budgeted revenues and the gradual decrease of extra budgeted revenues occurred to the structure of revenues obtained by the government of Chang'an District, which have been revealed by following details:

(1) Regarding the revenues structure of the government, budgeted revenues became the major component, a substitute for funds and extra budgeted revenues. The proportion of the budgeted portion to total revenues increased from 46% in 1999 to 62% in 2003, while that of the extra budgeted portion decreased from 42 to 31% during the same period.
(2) Budgeted revenues increased remarkably with a growth rate of 45% in 2002 and 24% in 2003, much higher than those of GDP during the same period (viz.18.5 and 13%, respectively).

What was the cause of such changes? Let's look at the composition of budgeted revenues.

Statistics show that dramatic changes had occurred to the structure of fiscal revenues during the five years. The most important three items of taxation for Chang'an District, namely VAT, business tax and agricultural tax, accounted for 13, 31 and 19% respectively of the budgeted revenues in 1999, while in 2003, these three proportions were changed to 7, 56 and 18% respectively. Although the proportion of agricultural tax was basically the same, the VAT dropped by 5, and the business tax of the same period went up by 25%, accounting for more than half of the total budgeted revenues.

If we take the data of 1999 as the base, the average annual growth rates of the business tax and urban construction tax would go up to 81 and 44% respectively, both higher than that of local budgeted revenues (33%).

The analysis above shows that the rapid increase of business tax was in sharp contrast with the slow increase or gradual decrease VAT and business income tax illustrating, to a certain degree, the slack industrialization in Chang'an District. As the business tax was only levied on the building industry in the secondary industry, a preliminary judgment can be made that the growth of fiscal revenues was mainly driven by the building industry and the tertiary industry.

Now let's make an industry-based review of the growth of fiscal revenues. In 1999, the most contributive industries with respect to local revenues were construction (34%), wholesale and retail trade (23%), and financial sector (15%), while in 2003, they were replaced by construction (61%), real estate (11%), and transportation (7%).

An industry-based review of the fiscal revenues reveals that:

(1) Fiscal revenues have become more and more dependent on construction and real estate sectors. Compared with the data of 1999, taxes levied on the construction sector had sextupled in 2003, while those on other sectors in the secondary industry barely doubled. In particular, taxes on the real estate sector, which had been a rising star in the local budgeted revenues, had increased by 19 times during this period.
(2) Structural changes mostly took place in 2002 and 2003 when the construction and real estate sectors expanded rapidly.

That the construction and real estate sectors had become the major source of local tax revenues features the economic development in Chang'an District. The total tax revenues in 2003 doubled if compared with those of 2001. Taxes on the construction and real estate sectors accounted for 96.7% of this increment, indicating that these two sectors had replaced industrialization and most other sectors of the tertiary industry in stimulating the growth of tax revenues. It can be preliminarily inferred from the changes in the tax structure that the economic growth in Chang'an District had relied heavily on requisition and demolition-centered construction expansion, rather than industrialization or urbanization marked by the development of the tertiary industry. In this mode of development, land of course plays a fundamental role.

Regarding the tax structure, this mode is characterized by a rapid increase in not only business tax on construction, but also other indirect and direct taxes levied on land in a broader sense. The proportion of direct taxes on land to local budgeted revenues increased from 3.4% in 1999 to 9.6% in 2003. Indirect taxes on land (in particular, business tax on constructors and real estate developers) also witnessed a rapid growth, especially in 2002 and 2003. The proportion of land tax to fiscal revenues increased from 22.7% in 1999 to 57.5% in 2003. Thus, it can be concluded that land and direct/indirect taxes on land are vital to the growth of budgeted fiscal revenues of Chang'an District.

As the tax-based budgeted revenues have been analyzed above, we will present a review of funds and extra budgeted revenues.

Funds and extra budgeted revenues decreased in proportion to the total fiscal revenues of the government of Chang'an District from 54% in 1999 to merely 38% in 2003. These non-tax revenues can be divided into three categories based on our purpose of analyzing land revenues: (a) land use right transfer fees; (b) land-related revenues; and (c) land-unrelated charges. The first category has been defined explicitly, while the other two might be difficult to distinguish in view of their numerous items as well as different departments involved. What makes the situation intricate is that some items do not belong to one category completely, for instance,

(a) the land use right transfer fees, limited in total sum as it is, had been subject to salient fluctuations in view of its year-on-year growth rate. And
(b) we cannot ascertain the scope of land-related charges, but we can get a general idea of it.

Administrative surcharges and incomes from government-managed funds are the major components of extra budgeted revenues of local governments. Incomes from government-managed funds obtained by the Government of Chang'an District mainly included three sub-categories, namely, toll charges, added urban education fund, and fees of supporting measures of urban construction directly related to land development which were considered by the Government of Chang'an District as one of the major capital sources for urban development and construction. As the most substantive among these three sub-categories, fees of supporting measures had been levied in full amount on all planning projects within the planned area. As toll charges and the added urban education fund were included in budget and thus considered as part of the budgeted revenues, the aforesaid fees of supporting measures for urban construction constituted the main bulk of government-managed funds in statistics, amounting to CNY 9.04 million, 14.88 million and 27.72 million in 2001, 2002 and 2003 respectively (up to CNY 50 million in total).

Due to the wide range of service charging sectors of administrative units and public institutions, it is difficult to tell which is related to land development and which is not. In fact, the latter two categories, viz. (b) and (c), can be hardly separated. According to the statistics, the proportion of the sum of land use right transfer fees and fees of supporting measures for urban construction (with miscellaneous charge excluded) to non-tax revenues notably increased from 20% before 2002 to 40% in 2003.

Based on the analysis above, it can be concluded that the fiscal revenues of the Government of Chang'an District had the following features:

Firstly, the budgeted revenues (or tax revenues) were attached with greater importance than non-tax revenues. In the past five years, the proportion of tax revenues went up from 40 to 60%, while that of the non-tax revenues dropped from 60 to 40%.

Secondly, the rapid growth of tax revenues was a result of land development, urban demolition and construction expansion, rather than the tertiary industry driven by industrialization and urbanization, as illustrated by the following facts: (1) there was barely any increase in the industrial tax, which exposed the slow progress of industrialization; (2) taxes on the tertiary industry (except those on the real estate sector) increased slowly, which manifestated the slow progress of population urbanization; and (3) 95% of the revenues increment was sourced from taxes on construction and real estate sectors, indicating that local economic development was almost completely motivated by land development. Based on this discovery, it can be inferred that under this economic growth model, inadequate industrialization and population urbanization were offset by high land urbanization.

Finally, land development has brought about an immediate growth of land revenues, but the direct incomes from land operation by the government, viz. the land use right transfer fees, have been diminishing. According to the statistics, it totaled CNY 7.9 million, 0.55 million and 24.59 million in the past three years respectively, merely accounting for 38, 0.2 and 7.1% of the fiscal revenues.

2. Land Finance of Shaoxing County

Shaoxing County is under the jurisdiction of Shaoxing City, Zhejiang Province. As the most economically developed area in the city representative of developed counties and cities in East China, it has ranked among the top ten of the top 100 counties for many years.

According to our survey data, the proportion of direct and indirect taxes on land to local budgeted revenues increased from 30.5% in 2001 to 38.4% in 2003, and a third of the budgeted financial resources of Shaoxing County were sourced from land revenues. It is worth noting that these taxes had risen much faster than other items and thus become the most important momentum for the growth of local fiscal revenues. From 2001 to 2003, the income tax on construction and real estate sectors decreased or stagnated, while the business tax thereon witnessed extremely rapid growth (the growth rates in 2002 and 2003 were 100 and 40% respectively), and so did the real estate tax. This is an odd phenomenon, for both the business tax and income tax should had risen rapidly if construction and real estate sectors expanded significantly in the past three years. The reason behind such a phenomenon lied in that only 40% of the income tax (in contrast with 100% of the business tax) were paid to the local government, which certainly dampened the enthusiasm of the local government in enhancing the income tax.

According to our survey, local fiscal revenues increased at a rate of 7.1% in 2002 and 28.1% in 2003, and the land revenues at 28.2 and 69.6% respectively, much higher than the former. The contribution rates of land revenues to the increment of total revenues were 109.9 and 71.3% respectively during the same period, which means that the growth of local fiscal revenues was principally driven by the increase in land revenues, echoing the situation of Chang'an District as discussed earlier (except for the extra budgeted portion).

Sources of extra budgeted revenues mainly included the land use right transfer fees and charges by various departments (including charges by land administration departments, land-related charges by other authorities, and charges unrelated to land). Our survey indicates that land-related charges constituted the major component of extra budgeted revenues.

The extra budgeted revenues obtained by the Government of Shaoxing County included administrative fees, government-managed funds, and the land use right transfer fees. Partial administrative fees were charged on land transfer and thus could be hardly distinguished. The IFAD and social security fund, which were the most substantive of government-managed funds, were appropriated as per the proportion of incomes from land transfer, thereby considered as part of land revenues. The land use right transfer fees should amount to the total revenues from land transfer. So, the aforesaid funds as well as the land use right transfer fees may roughly be deemed as the government's extra budgeted revenues from land. According to our survey data, land revenues accounted for more than 80% of the extra budgeted revenues.

As the comprehensive review of the situations in Chang'an District and Shaoxing County indicates, land revenues were undoubtedly the mainstay of local fiscal revenues. In Shaoxing County, both budgeted and extra budgeted land revenues were the most significant components of the fiscal revenues. This fiscal structure has been shaped by both exogenous and endogenous factors. Exogenous factors refer to the current land, finance and tax systems, while endogenous factors are the benefit-seeking behaviors of the local government under the current system. Under the tax-sharing system, the central government staked out the main body items of taxation within general budget for itself, leaving other items to local governments. In 2002, the central government determined that the business income tax and personal income tax, originally paid to local governments, should be shared between them in view of the rapid growth of such taxes since 1994. These measures of centralizing financial resources had generated a squeezing effect on the revenues of local governments so that the scattered minor items of taxation were gradually highlighted in their pursuit of revenues proliferation. As a result, since 2002 when it had been determined that the income tax should be shared with the central government, resulting in the rapid growth of the business tax. The business tax has played the most important role in enhancing local fiscal revenues ever since, which is the consequence of the "squeezing effect".

Under the tax-sharing system, the central government also made an attempt to reform the budget system. This reform was accomplished by submitting extra budgeted funds to budget control, implementing the centralized payment by national treasury and "keeping revenues and expenditures on two lines" for extra budgeted funds, with the aim of making revenues and expenditures transparent and standardizing their management. Considering the difference between budgeted funds that were subject to centralized and transparent management and extra budgeted funds under the relatively autonomous control, to submit extra budgeted funds to budget control would certainly confine the expenditures authority of local governments. This would result in the second "squeezing effect" forcing local governments to try their best to enhance extra-budgetary revenues originally excluded from budget control, while the most important component of these revenues was land revenues notably from the land use right transfer fees.

As the previous paragraph points out, local governments were "squeezed" and stimulated by the central fiscal policy. Regarding the local finance, the growth point of budgeted revenues has shifted to the business tax and land revenues under the dual "squeezing" effects, while the increment of extra budgeted revenues most notably relied on the land use right transfer fees. As shown in the analysis above, their growth rates have been among the highest in recent years.

Budgeted fiscal expenditures have been maintained under normal allotment, so it will not be discussed in details. Our analysis will focus on the utilization measures of the land use right transfer fees which mainly include the following.

Above all, the costs of land development and transfer including compensations for farmers and costs of water/power supply, access road and ground leveling (or plus gas and communications) may be paid with it. These expenditures are excluded from the net incomes from the land use right transfer fees and shall be appropriated to meet the following two ends.

First, to supplement fiscal expenditures and cover other costs of land requisition. Free from budget constraints, the land use right transfer fees is the "spare money" at the disposal of local governments. Its expenditures system was totally different from the standard one, with a considerable part appropriated by competent financial departments. Land requisition or transfer by the government has three primary purposes, i.e., public welfare, industrialization and operational purposes, subject to subdivision, agreement or auction respectively. Costs of land transfer for public welfare (road, water conservancy, education, health, etc.) could not even be covered by revenues, thereby entailing the necessity of a subsidy from the government. Second, there has also no profit for the government in the development of industrial land, for definite constraints would be imposed on the prices of land in order to attract investment. Therefore, the prices of industrial land would not keep increasing like commercial land, but it would be maintained steady to approximately cover development costs. And in some cases, a subsidy from the government might be necessary. During the process of land requisition and transfer, only operational land for commercial purposes is profitable for the government. Generally speaking, the transfer price and costs of land development for industrial purposes basically stay even. If the land is used for commercial purposes, the former would far exceed the latter. As for those lands transferred for public welfare, the costs of land requisition shall be (partially) covered by the net incomes from the land use right transfer fees.

Second, the majority of the land use right transfer fees shall be used as the basic assets to cover the high expenditures incurred by the establishment of government-run development and construction enterprises. Under the county-level government, there are usually some government-run enterprises engaged in urban investment and development, urban traffic investment, urban water industry, urban village reconstruction, etc. These investment enterprises commonly known as "government-invested enterprises" mostly founded after 2000 usually invite the leaders of relevant governmental departments to chair the board of directors or to work as the general manager. All these enterprises are non-profit organizations except for transport enterprises that are mainly engaged in the investment and construction of urban public infrastructures.

It seems that all these funds would be used for urban public construction projects, but it was far from the truth. The government injected the land use right transfer fees into relevant enterprises as the principle necessary for bank loans in its attempt at raising funds for constructing the city instead of direct city construction. In other words, the land use right transfer fees injected to enterprises by the government are used as capital funds for procuring bank loans, so they would not be spent on city construction directly. These government-run enterprises, commonly known as "financing platforms for local governments" were the key to connecting land finance The relationship between land fianance and urbanization will be discussed in the last section of this chapter. Next we will focus on a data-based empirical analysis of the close relationship between the tax system and land finance.

4.3 An Empirical Study of the Relationship Between the Tax System and Land Finance

Our empirical study of the relationship between the tax system and land fiannce will be based on China's existing macro-data disclosed by relevant statistics publications and panel data at the provincial level.

The basic hypothesis to be verified originated from the mechanism analysis in Chaps. 2, 3, and 4 which can be summarized as follows: under the new fiscal system, the more a local government lost, the more eager it would be to pursue benefits from land requisition, development and transfer. That is to say, since the implementation of the tax-sharing system and thereafter, the more the central government "took" from local governments, the more local governments would obtain from land requisition.

The main purpose of this subsection is to explain the inter-local government differences in their land expropriation behaviors. According to the analysis of incomes from the perspective of land expropriation by local governments conducted by Liu Shouying, Zhou Feizhou, et al., although there were also other revenues from "land operation" available to local governments, the land use right transfer fees was actually the largest in amount. Therefore, the dependent variable is defined as the amount of this fund.

Based on this hypothesis, under the new fiscal system, the more the central government took from local governments, the more radical the land acquisition behaviors of local governments would be. Therefore, taxes centralized by the central government became the core independent variable. Under the tax-sharing system implemented in 1994, 100% of the consumption duty and 75% of the VAT should be turned over to the central governments. As a result of the income tax reform in 2002, 50% of both the business income tax and the personal income tax were centralized. The percentage was 60% after 2002. Revenues centralized in these two fiscal reforms (referred to as tax loss of local governments in the reform of the fiscal system) may be obtained by deducting tax rebates from the sum of these centralized revenues. The calculation formula is as follows:

(1) Tax loss (before 2002) = (Consumption duty + VAT × 0.75)—Rebates of consumption duty and VAT;
(2) Tax loss (in 2002) = (Consumption duty + VAT × 0.75)—Rebates of consumption duty and VAT + (Business income tax + Personal income tax) 0.50—Income tax base rebates; and
(3) Tax loss (after 2002) = (Consumption duty + VAT × 0.75)—Rebates of consumption duty and VAT + (Business income tax + Personal income tax) 0.60—Income tax base rebates.

The control variables in this model include population, GDP, industrialization level (proportion of the secondary industry to GDP), urbanization level (proportion of non-agricultural population), etc. All variables other than industrialization and urbanization levels (expressed as percentage) are written in natural logarithms (ln). For the description of all the variables, please see the tables (Tables 4.1 and 4.2)

Let y_{it} be the amount of land use right transfer fees of Province i in the year of t, and X_{it} the tax loss.

$$y_{it} - y_{it-1} = -\alpha y_{it-1} + \beta' X_{it} + u_{it} \quad t = 1, 2, \ldots, T$$
$$u_{it} = \eta_i + w_t + \varepsilon_{it}$$
$$\beta = \alpha\pi, \quad \eta_i = \alpha\lambda_i, \quad w_t = \alpha\gamma_t, \quad \varepsilon_{it} = \alpha v_{it}$$

π is a parameter vector, while λ_i denotes a unique time-varying feature of Province i (such as the geographical location of a province) and γ_t a unique time-varying feature of year t (such as a decision on land requisition made by the central government in a certain year). The v_{it} in the formula represents a residual error. The following estimation methods will be adopted:

Table 4.1 Descriptive statistics of variables used in our analysis

	Observed value	Mean value	Standard deviation	Minimum value	Maximum value
Land use right transfer fees (ln)	308	12.04	1.95	6.22	16.28
Tax loss (ln)	309	13.27	1.66	6.29	16.78
Population (ln)	308	17.19	0.92	14.67	18.54
GDP (ln)	310	7.73	1.09	4.02	10.02
Urbanization level (%)	308	30.80	15.39	13.52	84.46
Industrialization level (%)	310	44.04	7.95	17.59	59.50

Table 4.2 Mean values of variables used in our analysis (differing by the year)

Year	Land use right transfer fees (ln)	Tax loss (ln)	Population (ln)	GDP (ln)	Urbanization level (%)	Industrialization level (%)
1995	10.86	12.21	17.15	7.14	27.98	42.98
1996	10.72	12.34	17.16	7.30	28.44	42.33
1998	11.20	12.56	17.17	7.50	28.86	42.61
1999	10.92	12.69	17.18	7.56	29.24	42.80
2000	11.13	13.07	17.19	7.66	29.73	43.59
2001	11.93	13.25	17.20	7.75	30.26	43.57
2002	12.67	13.72	17.21	7.85	31.41	43.91
2003	13.43	13.99	17.21	7.99	32.75	45.80
2004	13.76	14.33	17.22	8.17	34.04	47.34
2005	13.75	14.57	17.23	8.36	35.14	45.50
Total	12.04	13.27	17.19	7.73	30.80	44.04

(1) Ordinary least square. According to this method, the data of different provinces in different years are combined for estimation:

$$y_{it} - y_{it-1} = \beta' X_{it} + w_t + \tilde{u}_{it} \quad t = 1, 2, \ldots, T$$

(2) Random effects model (REM). Similar to the ordinary least square method, the random effects model also assumes the error term $(\tilde{\eta}_i + \tilde{\varepsilon}_{it})$ is unrelated to X_{it}. However, unobserved individual heterogeneity $(\tilde{\eta}_i)$ is excluded from this model.

$$y_{it} - y_{it-1} = \beta' X_{it} + w_t + (\tilde{\eta}_i + \tilde{\varepsilon}_{it}) \quad t = 1, 2, \ldots, T$$

(3) Fixed effects model (FEM). If the unobserved individual heterogeneity $\tilde{\eta}_i$ is related to X_{it}, there must be some missing variable (s), and the previous two methods would be biased and inconsistent. In this case, the fixed effects model can be used to eliminate the unobserved effects:

$$y_{it} - y_{it-1} = -\alpha y_{it-1} + \beta' X_{it} + w_t + n_i + \tilde{\varepsilon}_{it} \quad t = 1, 2, \ldots, T$$

(4) Difference-GMM. y_{it-1} is ignored in the three methods mentioned above. If y_{it-1} is uncontrolled in the regression equation, estimates will be biased and inconsistent, so we need to apply the generalized method of moments to estimate the equation. In this method, the fixed effects may be eliminated by first-order difference, and then $y_{it-p}(p \geq 2)$ is used as an instrumental variable to correct the difference:

$$y_{it} = (1 - \alpha)y_{it-1} + \beta' X_{it} + u_{it} \quad t = 1, 2, \ldots, T$$

(5) System-GMM. This method uses $\Delta y_{it-p}(p \geq 2)$ as an instrumental variable to correct the endogeneity of the lagged variable of the dependent variable $(y_{it-l}, l \geq 1)$:

$$\begin{aligned} y_{it} &= (1 - \alpha)y_{it-1} + \sum_{l=2}^{L} \rho_l y_{it-1} + \beta' X_{it} + u_{it} \quad t = 1, 2, \ldots, T \\ u_{it} &= \eta_i + w_t + \varepsilon_{it} \end{aligned} \tag{4.1}$$

Estimate results of the pedestal OLS method are listed in Table 4.3. We inserted independent variables into the four equations in the following order: First, core independent variable (Eq. 4.1); Second, control variable (Eq. 4.2); Third, virtual variable of years (Eq. (4.3); Fourth, virtual variable of regions (Eq. 4.4). In all of the models, the core variable, viz. tax loss, is extremely significant and positive, which is consistent with our hypothesis—the greater the tax loss incurred to a provincial government in the reform of the fiscal system was, the more eager it would be in its pursuit of revenues from the land use right transfer fees. By calculating the marginal effects of this variable, we can see that every additional 1% of tax losses incurred to local governments in the fiscal system reform would motivate them to gain 0.5–1% more from local land transfer in order to cover the aforesaid losses.

Table 4.3 Regression results of the OLS method

	Dependent variable: land use right transfer fees (ln)			
	1	2	3	4
Tax loss (ln)	0.998***	0.834***	0.572***	0.513***
	(0.034)	(0.081)	(0.084)	(0.086)
Population (ln)		−1.417***	−1.173***	−0.560***
		(0.146)	(0.157)	(0.210)
GDP (ln)		1.554***	1.645***	1.096***
		(0.174)	(0.164)	(0.223)
Urbanization level (%)		−0.043***	−0.031***	−0.019***
		(0.005)	(0.006)	(0.006)
Industrialization level (%)		−0.040***	−0.039***	−0.031***
		(0.008)	(0.007)	(0.007)
Virtual variable of years			√	√
Virtual variable of regions				√
Constant term	−1.202***	16.438***	14.778***	8.548***
	(0.455)	(1.855)	(1.916)	(2.354)
Observed value	307	307	307	307
R^2	0.739	0.825	0.865	0.873

***$p < 0.01$; ** $p < 0.05$; * $p < 0.\ 1$. The values in brackets are standard errors

The results of the REM and FEM methods are listed in Table 4.4. Consistent with those of the OLS method, the results of the FEM show that every additional 1% of tax losses incurred to local governments in the fiscal system reform would motivate them to gain 0.74% more from local land transfer (see Eq. 4.4 in Table 4.4).

The generalized matrix method (GMM) shall satisfy two conditions: first, the error term ε_a is unrelevant; second, the instrumental variable is exogenous. Results of the difference-GMM are listed in Table 4.5. The first condition of this method is that the first order difference $\Delta\varepsilon_a$ of the error term must be significant in first-order serial correlation while insignificant in second-order serial correlation. m_1 and m_2 are used to verify this condition. The results listed in Table 4.5 show that the first condition of the generalized matrix method is satisfied; and, as indicated by the value of p in Hansen tests, the second is also satisfied.

Since the generalized matrix method will generate a large number of instrumental variables, a limited sample may be unable to estimate a large matrix accurately, which will lead to model over-identification and weakened Sargan/Hansen tests and a failure to obtain $p = 1.000$. According to Eqs. 4.1 and 4.2, although $p = 1.000$ is not obtained satisfactorily in Sargan/Hansen tests, the number of instrumental variables (25) does not exceed that of cross-sectional units (namely, 31 provinces). As shown by Eqs. 4.3 and 4.4, when other variables are controlled, even though the number of instrumental variable (65) exceeds that of cross-sectional units (31), $p = 1.000$ may be obtained in Hansen tests. In conclusion, the estimate results of the difference-GMM model are acceptable.

Table 4.4 Random Effect model and fixed effect model

	Dependent variable: land use right transfer fees (ln)			
	1	2	3	4
	Random effect		Fixed effect	
Tax loss (ln)	0.795***	0.654***	0.587***	0.737***
	(0.068)	(0.114)	(0.136)	(0.135)
Population (ln)		−0.978***		−5.431***
		(0.274)		(1.265)
GDP (ln)		1.241***		−1.246**
		(0.263)		(0.568)
Urbanization level (%)		−0.030***		−0.024
		(0.010)		(0.017)
Industrialization level (%)		−0.016		0.037**
		(0.011)		(0.016)
Constant term	1.146	12.286***	3.690***	103.057***
	(0.846)	(3.340)	(1.662)	(21.627)
Observed value	307	307	307	307
R^2			0.818	0.837
Number of provinces	31	31	31	31

***$p < 0.01$; **$p < 0.05$; *$p < 0.1$. The values in brackets are robust standard errors. The results of the virtual variable of years included in the equation is not reported

Tax loss is significant in almost all difference-GMM models (except for Eq. 4.4). Thus, our hypothesis is verified (Table 4.5).

The m_1 and m_2 as shown in the table are the statistical values of the first-order difference of error term in the first and second-order serial correlation respectively.

Sargan and Hansen tests are applied to verify whether the instrumental variable is exogenous. The results were represented as p in the table.

Estimate results of the system-GMM model are listed in Table 4.6. The results of m_1 and m_2 show that the first-order difference of the error term is significant in first-order serial correlation but insignificant in second-order serial correlation, which satisfies the first condition of the generalized matrix method. Meanwhile, as indicated by the value of p in Hansen tests, the second is also satisfied. According to Eqs. 4.1 and 4.2, although $p = 1.000$ is not obtained satisfactorily in Sargan/Hansen tests, the number of instrumental variables does not exceed that of cross-sectional units. As shown by Eqs. 4.3 and 4.4, when other variables are controlled, even though the number of instrumental variable exceeds that of cross-sectional units, $p = 1.000$ may be obtained in Hansen tests. In conclusion, the estimate results of the system-GMM model are reliable.

Table 4.5 Estimate results of the difference-GMM model

	Dependent variable: land use right transfer fees (ln)			
	1	2	3	4
	One-way	Two-way	One-way	Two-way
Tax loss (ln)	0.774 ***	0.740 ***	0.694 **	0.471
	(0.221)	(0.190)	(0.300)	(0.561)
Population (ln)			−11.046 *	1.19
			(6.087)	(9.624)
GDP (ln)			−3.051 ***	−2.116
			(0.834)	(1.565)
Urbanization level (%)			−0.028	−0.033
			(0.033)	(0.076)
Industrialization level (%)			0.081 **	0.11
			(0.038)	(0.082)
First-order lagged variable of the dependent variable	0.244 ***	0.247 ***	0.139 *	0.099
	(0.094)	(0.090)	(0.077)	(0.113)
Observed value	184	184	184	184
Number of provinces	31	31	31	31
m_1	−2.83	−2.15	−2.58	−1.98
m_2	−0.39	−0.31	−0.61	−0.5
Sargan test (value of p)	0.051	0.051	0.010	0.010
Hansen test (value of p)	0.629	0.629	1.000	1.000
Number of instrumental variables	25	25	65	65

***$p < 0.01$; **$p < 0.05$; *$p < 0.1$. The values in brackets are robust standard errors. The results of the virtual variable of years included in the equation is not reported

Table 4.6 Estimate Results of the System-GMM Model

	Dependent variable: Land use right transfer fees (ln)			
	1	2	3	4
	One-way	Two-way	One-way	Two-way
Tax loss (ln)	0.889 ***	0.850 ***	0.356 **	1.195 **
	(0.202)	(0.191)	(0.169)	(0.599)
Population (ln)			−0.233	−5.647
			(0.421)	(6.719)
GDP (ln)			1.040 **	0.376
			(0.472)	(0.751)
Urbanization level (%)			−0.017	0.019
			(0.017)	(0.048)
Industrialization level (%)			−0.027	0.05
			(0.020)	(0.059)
First-order lagged variable of the dependent variable	0.177	0.181	0.219 **	0.163
	(0.123)	(0.116)	(0.107)	(0.125)
Constant term	−1.642	−1.105	2.685	85.728
	(4.005)	(3.609)	(4.092)	(107.081)
Observed value	246	246	246	246
Number of provinces	31	31	31	31
	1	2	3	4
m_1	−2.4	−1.97	−2.42	−1.7
m_2	−0.62	−0.57	−0.44	−0.56
Sargan test (value of p)	0.000	0.000	0.000	0.000
Hansen test (value of p)	0.616	0.616	1.000	1.000
Number of instrumental variables	29	29	73	73

***$p < 0.01$; ** $p < 0.05$; * $p < 0.1$. The values in brackets are robust standard errors. The results of the virtual variable of years included in the equation is not reported

In all of the 4 equations of the system-GMM, the core variable, viz. tax loss, is extremely significant at 0.05 and positive, which is consistent with our hypothesis again. In Eq. 4, the coefficient of this variable is 1.195, suggesting that every additional 1% of tax losses incurred to local governments in the fiscal system reform would drive them to gain 1.2% more from local land transfer.

The m_1 and m_2 as shown in the table are the statistical values of the first-order difference of error term in the first and second-order serial correlation respectively.

Sargan and Hansen tests are applied to verify whether the instrumental variable is exogenous. What are reported in the table are the values of p.

Our hypothesis is verified by the results of all models listed in Tables 4.3, 4.4, 4.5 and 4.6 from different perspectives, namely, the greater the loss incurred to local governments in the reform of the fiscal system was, the more eager they would be in their pursuit of revenues from land transfer. Moreover, the results are robust in all estimate models, manifestating the reliability of our hypothesis.

Chapter 5
Land Planning Quotas

Ever since the tax-sharing reform, the fiscal and political performance of local governments has become more and more dependent on land and city operation. Land has become the core element of local development. Without land, there can be no development at all. "It is even more difficult to obtain land approval than to ascend to heaven. Money can buy gold, but land is priceless". However, under the current land system, local governments are universally faced with difficulties as a result of the inconsistency between the central government and local governments in their attitudes toward land requisition, development and transfer. The central government should give considerations to not only the role of land development in promoting economic growth, but also its negative impacts on farmland protection, food security and social stability. Hence, the high demand on land of local governments has been always confronted with stringent measures imposed by the central government. Such land issues highlight the inconsistency between the comprehensive target of farmland protection, food security, economic growth and social stability on the one hand and the single-minded pursuit of rapid economic growth on the other. However, unrelenting strict control would undoubtedly make a dent in the initiative of local governments and, in turn, endanger the authority of the central government when "gray" and even illegal land use cases take place. Both parties have been involved in a series of games on land. From the perspective of the central government, the single-minded control is obviously unsustainable, making policy easing inevitable. Thus, the "synchronism of control and stimulation" has featured the relationship between the central government and local governments, especially when involved in land issues. This chapter attempts to comb the policies made the central government for various land management systems and focus on the transition from balance between occupying and compensation to linking increase of increase of urban construction land and decrease of rural residential land so as to examine the basic situation of trade-off between the central government and local governments with respect to land issues.

F. Zhou and M. Tan, *Relationship between the Central Government and Local Governments of Contemporary China*, Social Development Experiences in China,
DOI 10.1007/978-981-10-4388-8_5

5.1 Land Management System

A strict land management system is implemented in China, whereby the primary land market is monopolized by the government. As land treasury played an increasingly important role in recent years, farmland non-agriculturalization has stimulated the pursuit of interests maximization by local governments. As provided in Article 43 of the *Land Administration Law of the PRC*, all units and individuals that need land for construction shall, in accordance with law, apply for the use of state-owned land, with the exception of the collective economic organizations and farmers of such organizations that have lawfully obtained approval of using the land owned by the farmer collective of the organizations to build township or town enterprises or to build houses for villagers and the units and individuals that have lawfully obtained approval of using the land owned by a farmer collective to build public utilities or public welfare undertakings for a township (town) or village, which means that all land to be used for construction shall be subject to ownership transfer to the State before appropriation or transfer in the name of the State. Statistics show that since 2000, China's newly added urban construction land has been mainly obtained by means of requisition, and the primary land market or land use right has been completely monopolized by the State. Revenues from farmland non-agriculturalization were mostly retained by local governments, leading to their pursuit of interests maximization (Table 5.1).

Table 5.1 Proportion of requisitioned land to newly added construction land from 2000 to 2011 in China (*unit* square km, %)

Year	Area of urban construction land	Area of newly added urban construction land	Area of requisitioned land	Proportion of requisitioned land to newly added construction land (%)
2000	22113.7	1236.7	447.49	36.18
2001	24192.7	2079	1813.11	87.21
2002	26832.6	2639.9	2881.31	109.14
2003	28971.9	2139.3	1606.4	75.09
2004	30781.3	1809.4	1613.34	89.16
2005	29636.8	−1145	1264.17	−110.5
2006	34166.7	4529.9	1397.16	30.84
2007	36351.7	2185	1216.61	55.68
2008	39140.46	2788.8	1345.27	48.24
2009	38726.9		1504.7	
2010	39758.4		1641.6	
2011	41860.6		1841.7	

Data source China Urban Construction Statistical Yearbook (2000–2012); *China Statistical Yearbook* (2000–2012)

Note The area of urban construction land in 2005 listed in the table above does not include those in Beijing and Shanghai

From the perspective of the relationship between the central government and local governments, the central government, with its final monopoly over land in the top-bottom land target control, issues general/annual land use plans with the view of an overall control over the construction land of local governments at various levels. The current overall land plans can be divided into five levels according to the effectiveness level and the administrative authority of the preparer(s), namely the national, provincial (or autonomous region/municipality direct under the central government), municipal, county and township (town) levels. The overall plan for land utilization at a lower level shall be drawn up on the basis of such a plan drawn up at the next higher level. The total area of land for construction in the overall plan for land utilization drawn up by local people's governments at different levels shall not exceed the control norm set in such a plan by the people's government at the next higher level and the area of cultivated land reserved shall not be smaller than the control norm set in the overall plan for land utilization of the people's government at the next higher level. As a result, the local competition tended towards a planning competition to a large extent. An annual land use plan shall include specific arrangements and targets provided by the State for the areas of newly added construction land, cultivated land to be developed, consolidated or compensated, and/or retained within the planned program. The Ministry of Land and Resources shall submit its request to the State Council in order to determine the planned annual national target for land use, which will be then issued to relevant the provincial (autonomous region), municipal and county authorities of land and resources level by level. Planning targets for newly added construction land that are vital for local development are subject to mandatory management and shall not be violated. Regarding the protection of cultivated land, the central government implemented strict monitoring on agricultural land transfer so that the "capital farmland protection rate" may be maintained. It is provided in Article 35 of the *Land Administration Law of the PRC* that the capital farmland designated as such by all provinces, autonomous regions and municipalities directly under the Central Government shall account for at least 80% of the total cultivated land in their administrative regions respectively, and the planned urban construction land shall be outside the capital farmland protection zone, imposing a severe confinement on local governments (Fig. 5.1).

In the cycle of land, treasury and finance, land is the core element on which the other two are based. However, under the background of rapid industrialization and urbanization, local governments, especially those in the eastern coastal areas, are all faced with a shortage of available land. In particular, the central governments has implemented strict control over land since 2006, so the annual target for newly added construction land could hardly satisfy the demand of development from local governments, leaving a large number of projects "waiting" for target approval. It is disclosed by the State Information Center that from 2000 to 2010, China's urban population increased by around 200 million, and the area of urban construction land increased by 117,600 *mu* (1 *mu* $\approx$ 666.7 m^2); by 2030, urbanization and industrialization will be basically completed; by then, the urbanization rate will reach 70%, which will need to displace 300 million people and non-agriculturalize 40

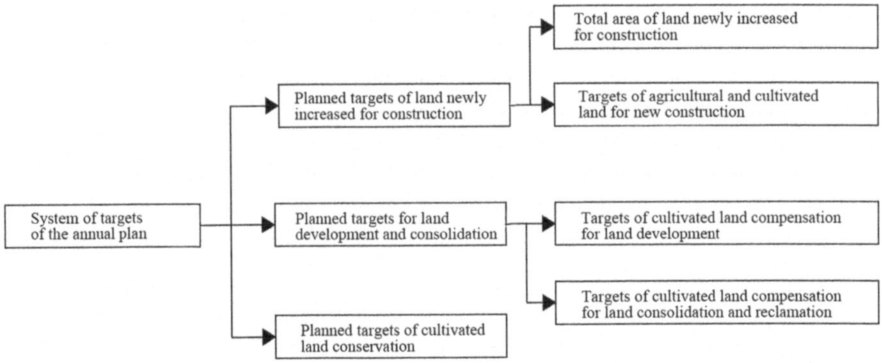

Fig. 5.1 System of annual planning targets for land use

年度计划指标体系：System of targets of the annual plan

新增建设用地计划指标：Planned targets of land newly increased for construction

土地开发整理计划指标：Planned targets for land development and consolidation

耕地保有量计划指标：Planned targets of cultivated land conservation

新增建设用地总量：Total area of land newly increased for construction

新增建设占农用地及耕地指标：Targets of agricultural and cultivated land for new construction

土地开发补充耕地指标：Targets of cultivated land compensation for land development

土地整理复垦补充耕地指标：Targets of cultivated land compensation for land consolidation and reclamation

million *mu* of land". How can we make up the 40 million *mu* of land is an issue to be addressed by the central government as well as local governments. What is even more urgent is that local governments have been more dependent on and thus attached greater importance to financing in face of increased demand on investment and fiscal expenditures since 2008. In June 2010, the State Council embarked on a liquidation of the financing platforms of local government, confining their credit guarantee financing behaviors. As a result of the ever-increasing demands on financing, land mortgage-based financing was increasingly favored by both governments at the municipal and county levels and financial institutions. Land finance that evolved from land treasury became wide-spread in China. Regarding the urgent demands on land, the focus gradually shifted from land resources for construction projects to fiscal revenues from land selling, which is known as land financing.

In view of the strict land control by the central government, it is urgent to give full play to the newly added construction land. For local governments, land targets provide top-down control and stimulation simultaneously in this sense: on the one hand, the annual planning targets in terms of retention of cultivated land shall be accomplished; on the other hand, the central government shall determine the planning targets in terms of the area of newly added construction land each year, so that all construction projects may be confined by relevant targets. In the existing development mode, the latter will undoubtedly impose high confinement on local governments, because land is the basis of development, and without quotas for newly added construction land, any revenues from land would be deemed illegal. In such a context, the central government and local governments have been involved in repeated games on "land targets".

5.2 Balancing Cultivated Land and Compensation: A Passive and Strict Control

Considering the increasingly fast-paced industrialization and urbanization ever since the reform and opening up, it is inevitable that vast cultivated farmland would be occupied in the process of national development. In particular, since the beginning of the 21st century, the pursuit of land finance of local governments has brought about nationwide demolition and construction, accompanied by a sharp increase of land-lost farmers and frequent mass incidents endangering social stability. In response to the requirements of the basic operation and organization mode with the view of safeguarding national food security and maintaining the household contract responsibility system that has been implemented ever since the reform, the protection system for cultivated land has been strictly implemented, and thus a series of policies represented by balancing arable land occupation and compensation arose at the historic moment. As a political task, 1.8 billion *mu* of cultivated land should be retained, for which the leaders of the competent authorities shall be responsible.

A basic national policy that calls for us to "treasure and put every inch of land to rational utilization, and protect arable land practically" is proposed in *Notice on Strengthening Land Management and Preventing Unauthorized Arable Land Occupation* (No. 7) as promulgated by State Council in March, 1986, foreshadowing the introduction of the cultivated land balance system. As approved by the standing committee of the 6th National People's Congress (NPC) on June 25, 1986, the *Land Administration Law of the PRC* was promulgated and took effect as of the same date. In April 1997, the State Council issued *Notice on Further Strengthening Land Management and Preventing Unauthorized Arable Land Occupation* (No. 11), which explicitly stipulates that each province (autonomous region/ municipality) shall maintain a dynamic balance of total cultivated land and provides the policy of integrating cultivated land occupation and development/reclamation. Thus, the concept of "cultivated land balance" was proposed for the first time. It is also pointed out that land management and protection of cultivated land are vital for the overall situation as well as the coming generations of China, so it is required to take stringent measures and implement the aforementioned basic national policy—

treasure and put every inch of land to rational utilization, and protect arable land practically, so as to put an end to the imbalance between ever-decreasing cultivated land and ever-increasing population. According to the amendment to the *Land Administration Law of the PRC* in August 1998, the "compensation system for occupying cultivated land" shall be implemented in order to balance the occupation and development and/or reclamation of cultivated land. The *Land Administration Law of the PRC* as amended took effect on January 1, 1999, completed by the *Regulation on the Implementation of the Land Administration Law of the Peoples Republic of China* (1998) and *Regulation on the Protection of Basic Farmlands of the Peoples Republic of China* (1998). On February 4, 1999, the Ministry of Land and Resources issued the *Notice on Balancing Cultivated Land Occupation and Compensation*, which proposes full advance compensation for construction-oriented cultivated land occupation. Since then, this policy has been implemented nationwide. In simple terms, the occupied land and compensating land shall be equal in terms of area and quality in order to maintain the area of cultivated land in China at a steady level.

However, the biggest problem with the dynamic balance of cultivated land occupation and compensation before 2006 lied in the "overall accounting"-based or regional assessment. In this simple method, we only need to calculate the total occupied/newly added cultivated land in a certain region and thus may be relieved of the trouble of project-by-project examination, which is obviously defective. Seemingly, regional balance has been achieved, but a detailed examination would reveal that many construction projects failed in this regard, resulting in the disconnection of cultivated land compensation and development. At the same time, imbalance between cultivated land occupation and compensation was notable in some construction projects as attention was only paid to the area of land. According to the statistics, only 35% of the compensating cultivated land, in contrast with 67% of occupied cultivated land for construction, was provided with irrigation facilities in 2005. Thus, a more elaborate and more stringent management system was developed. In 2005, the Ministry of Land and Resources included the areas of retained cultivated land and capital farmland protection zone in the assessment indicators for governors, whereby the administrative leader should be responsible. Under the *Measures for the Examination on the Balance between the Occupation and Supplement of Arable Land* that was approved by the Ministry of Land and Resources at the 3rd ministerial affaires meeting on June 8, 2006 and implemented as of August 1, 2006, cultivated land balance assessment shall be conducted on how the land and resources administration authorities at or above the county level have implemented the compensation for transforming cultivated land into non-agricultural construction land legally according to the principle of "fully reclaiming the occupied cultivated land". This "brand-new assessment mechanism" is innovative in its transition from regional "overall accounting" to project-by-project examination and integration of cultivated land occupation-based construction projects and compensation-based land development and consolidation projects with the view that compensation may be fulfilled during the execution of land development and consolidation projects. More importantly, the overall accounting has been replaced by the separate project evaluation system. This idea has been carried on by the principle of linking increase of urban construction land and decrease of rural residential land or "closed operation" which, in turn, has an impact on the implementation of relevant policies, which will be discussed in details later.

However, industrialization and urbanization are what the times requires, so the "redline for cultivated land retention" has become a heavy political and financial burden for local governments. Since its introduction, the policy of balancing cultivated land occupation and compensation has been hampered by the following risks: virtual compensation for cultivated land occupation, compensating low-quality cultivated land for high-quality occupied cultivated land, cultivated land non-agriculturalization and non-grain tendency. In fact, the principle of advance compensation for occupying cultivated land for construction under the cultivated land balance system has been frequently violated, which, coupled with inadequate supervision over supplement cultivated land, further led to insufficient or even zero compensation for occupied cultivated land. According to the *Notice on Further Strengthening Land Consolidation, Reclamation and Development* promulgated by the Ministry of Land and Resources, advance compensation for occupied cultivated land for non-agricultural purposes shall be comprehensively implemented since 2009, except that deferment may be allowed in key projects of the State. Thus, newly added land for construction projects shall not be approved until occupied cultivated land is made up for, and the reclamation should be led by competent authorities of land and resources with the financial support of the construction unit(s). Since then, advance compensation for occupied cultivated land has been actually implemented, except that such compensation may be virtual. A national survey of land use shows that from 1996 to 2006, the total area of cultivated land decreased by 0.124 billion *mu*, from 1.951 billion *mu* in 1996 to 1.827 billion *mu* in 2006, and the per capita area of cultivated land was only 1.3 acres, 40% lower than the world's average level. In addition, the compensating cultivated land was usually located beyond the production and life radius of farmers, which has led to a failure to put such newly added cultivated land to contracted operations and stripped farmers of farmland, employment, money and minimum living standard security, adding risks to the social stability. Local governments are concerned about how to enhance benefits from land production, which can be hardly achieved under the original grain-dominated planting structure. Thus, farmland agriculturalization and non-grain tendency based production structure transformation became an inevitable choice. Moreover, food security was not a concern for local governments. At this point, the contradictions between the central government and local governments zoomed in. As mentioned by Chen Xiwen in an interview, "I have been to those major grain-producing provinces. The title "major grain-producing provinces" seemed unpleasing to them, because they also had an ardor for industrialization and urbanization which, however, are forbidden in major grain-producing provinces".

As the reclamation and consolidation of cultivated land take a certain period, the shift from post-compensation to advance compensation for occupied cultivated land thus ushered target-based standardization for cultivated land balance, setting of a rush for establishing target reserves. When the occupation of cultivated land is required by a new project, available targets may be appropriated from the reserves. However, land consolidation has become increasingly difficult, and the fallback cultivated land resources have also been ever-diminishing, which has greatly confined the capability of cultivated land replenishment. In particular, it has been even more difficult to achieve cultivated land balance in economically developed areas. In such a background emerged the realistic demands on inter-regional target transactions. As a result, the purchase of cultivated land balancing targets by economically developed regions as characterized by excessive occupation and limited fallback resources from economically undeveloped areas characterized by exactly the opposite has been especially popular. However, according to the provisions of the Ministry of Land and Resources, balancing cultivated land occupation and compensation is only allowed within the administrative area of a provincial unit, eliminating its possibilities at the inter-provincial level. Provinces in economically developed regions are usually confined by limited fallback cultivated land resources. For example, in Shandong Province, there are merely 1.65 million *mu* of fallback cultivated land resources, while the annual newly-added construction land reaches around 180,000 mu. So, the balance can be maintained for only 8–9 years as a result of the ever-decreasing developable land resources. It will be extremely difficult to maintain balance between legal cultivated land occupation and compensation. It is heard from the local authority that "we can only dig mountains if this tendency continues". Meanwhile, as the administrative areas within a provincial unit become more and more aware of the future potentials for development in land, even those areas abundant in fallback resources would draw back their land-selling hands, further exaggerating the shortage of targets. There are 7.92 million *mu* of undeveloped land in the Yellow River Delta in Dongying and Binzhou, including 4.82 million *mu* of developable land. Since February 2011, Dongying has concluded a series of target purchase agreements with Qingdao, Yantai, etc., under which targets for altogether 20,000 *mu* of land have been sold at CNY 600 million. However, such internal transactions came to an abrupt end in 2012.

5.2.1 Summary

In this subsection, we combed through the problems and difficulties in introducing and implementing the policy of balancing cultivated land occupation and compensation. Frankly speaking, these difficulties have embodied the inner tension that has been present in this policy from the outset. It is noted by an operator in a field project that "it is inevitable to occupy cultivated land for construction, but the limited resources and the continuity of economic development have determined that the balance of cultivated land in the traditional sense cannot be ensured in the long run". Ever since this policy came into force, the central government has imposed strict control over land. In the existing development mode, the land operation incentive mechanism for local governments remains active, so inevitably, the occupation of cultivated land will be carried on. In this process, the inconsistency between the comprehensive objective (namely, cultivated land protection, food security, and economic growth) of the central government and the single-minded pursuit of economic development as fast as possible by local governments will be magnified. Meanwhile, as the difficulties for local governments to balance cultivated land accumulate year by year, the existing cultivated land protection system centered on the balance of occupation and compensation as well as the land use target monitoring system will be faced with huge challenges.

In such a context, how to help local governments seek new "legal" land sources within the existing policy framework became a common concern for both the central government and local governments. From the perspective of policy makers, the consolidation of construction land that belongs to the rural collective has been a major approach to this end, based on the sharp contrast between ever-diminishing rural/agricultural population and ever-increasing construction land in rural areas. The construction land of a rural collective has mainly come from the house sites of farmers. On this basis, the policy of linking increase of urban construction land and decrease of rural residential land was promulgated.

5.3 Land Replacement and Conversion Quotas: A "Leeway" Under the Strict Control

Of course, the policy of linking increase of urban construction land and decrease of rural residential land is not a new idea conceived overnight or even dreamt up by the central land sector, but based on the accumulated pilot experiences in reform and refinement before it can be promoted and implemented nationwide, which is a key characteristic of the reform of China. In 1999, the Ministry of Land and Resources put forward two essential policies on the basis of summarizing the experiences in national land development and consolidation, namely land replacement and target conversion ratio of 60%, which can be considered as a tap opened by the central government in response to the booming demands of local governments on land within the framework of the land management system, a prelude to the introduction of the policy of linking increase of urban construction land and decrease of rural residential land.

The so-called land replacement policy is aimed at expediting the translocation of rural residents to central villages and towns and of township-run enterprises to industrial districts in accordance with requirements of the overall plan for land utilization and village/town planning. Should the selected resettlement site be on cultivated land, replacement with the original site through consolidation may provide a solution so that the land for construction does not need to take up the annual cultivated land planning target for construction. As further clarified in the *Notice of the Ministry of Land and Resources on Several Policies and Measures for*

Strengthening Cultivated Land Protection and Promoting Economic Development promulgated by Decree No. 408 in 2000, the policy of construction land target replacement provides that for the recultivation of rural residential sites or construction land owned by the township (town) or village collective, an application may be filed for adding targets of cultivated land occupation for construction on the strength of approval by competent departments of land and resources administration at the provincial level, with the view of relatively centralized rural construction land by expediting the translocation of rural residents to central villages and towns and of enterprises to industrial districts. The second policy corresponds to the provisions in Article 18 of the *Regulation on the Implementation of the Land Administration Law of the PRC* of 1999 that 60% of the area of the newly-added cultivated land through land arrangement may be used as compensation targets to compensate for the cultivated land occupied for construction. That is to say, where balance of cultivated land occupation and compensation is achieved, the local government may file an application with the competent department of land administration at the next higher level for a certain area of cultivated land reserve target for the local necessary non-agricultural construction by using 60% of the area of the newly-added cultivated land through land arrangement as compensation targets. According to the provisions in Decree No. 408 promulgated by the Ministry of Land and Resources in 2000, we shall actively promote the policy of agricultural land consolidation target conversion and encourage the consolidation of agricultural land. And in order to enhance the consolidation of agricultural land owned by the rural collective, each region shall independently raise money for such consolidation with the view of a net increase in the area of cultivated land, and on this basis, an application may be filed for increasing targets of cultivated land occupation for construction on the strength of approval by competent departments of land and resources administration at the provincial level with 60% of the area of the newly-added cultivated land. The arrangements for obtaining cultivated land targets for construction through conversion shall also be in line with the overall plan for land utilization.

Spared from taking up annual land targets for construction, land replacement and conversion were favored by local governments uniformly, for which pertinent policies were promulgated successively by Zhejiang, Shandong, Anhui, and other provinces. However, the central policy was obviously interpreted and applied in different ways. As early as before 1999 when the central policy was introduced, Zhejiang had made in-depth exploration on the compensation for construction land through consolidation. In June 1998, *Notice on Issues Related to Encouraging Rural Land Consolidation* was promulgated the People's Government of Zhejiang Province, with the view of using land consolidation capitalization as a solution to the shortage of incentives to governments at the municipal/county level in this regard. It was stipulated by the People's Government of Zhejiang Province that 72% of the area of the useful newly-added cultivated land through land arrangement could be used as compensation targets to compensate for the cultivated land occupied for construction. More specifically, in planning and preparing for the implementation of a land consolidation project, 30% of the useful newly-added cultivated land as expected could be used as advance compensation targets to compensate for the cultivated land that has to be occupied for construction of roads, utilities and relocated buildings during the consolidation process, which should be paid for at a rate of CNY 20,000/*mu* from the land use right transfer fees and used as the start-up capital for land consolidation. Upon the acceptance of the entire project, 60% of the remaining 70% of the newly added cultivated land, i.e., 42% of the newly added cultivated land in the project might be used to compensate for construction land. Therefore, altogether 72% of the newly added active cultivated land in the project could be used as conversion targets. This system not only satisfied those areas highly demanding on land for construction, but also helped to raise the start-up capital and thus eliminated the financial difficulties in land consolidation. Thus, two objectives were attained by this single move. A massive campaign of land consolidation was cranked up by the introduction of the conversion target system in Zhejiang. Of course, local governments usually tended to focus on the first objective. In 1999, by carrying out land consolidation in Longgang Town, Cangnan County towards establishing a modern agricultural park, more than 2000 *mu* of cultivated land was newly added, and the conversion targets reached 1400 *mu*, which were mostly used to compensate for urban construction, except those for rural infrastructure and residency. In Shaoxing County, the annual demand on land around 2002 was approximately 4000 *mu*, in contrast with less than 1000 *mu* of land target appropriated by the competent authority; since June 1998 when pilot land consolidation target conversion was introduced, more than 15,000 *mu* of effective cultivated land was newly added in 872 villages from 20 towns, and over 10,000 *mu* of cultivated land was allowed to be used as conversion targets, thereby eliminating the tension with land supply during the development process. More notably, the conversion target reserve for future urbanization even exceeded 2200 *mu*.

Similar to the occupation and compensation-balancing targets as discussed earlier, conversion targets were also involved in inter-regional transactions inevitably as a result of target-based standardization or marketized configuration of land resources that basically encouraged the purchase-based flow of land targets from economically developed areas to relatively undeveloped areas. For example, the People's Government of Zhejiang Province has allowed the inter-regional paid redistribution of conversion targets (reclamation targets inclusive) since 2000 in order to break the regional imbalance between supply and the demand of construction land. Therefore, it has become increasingly pervading that economically developed areas purchase conversion targets from relatively undeveloped areas so as to maintain the development. According to statistics, by the end of 2004, the newly added cultivated land and appropriated conversion target through land consolidation had reached 1.8207 and 1.3108 million *mu* respectively, and the area of cultivated land approved under conversion targets was 1.0426 million *mu*, accounting for 58% of the total approved cultivated land to be occupied for construction (1.7927 million *mu*). Targets marketization has ushered a very subtle change: the original land replacement and target conversion were principally aimed at promoting land consolidation to some extent still; however, as the target market expanded gradually, the increasing demand on land from economically developed areas has become the core factor to be considered in policy making. The relatively less developed areas began to base their land consolidation on the interests from land selling, forfeiting their pursuit of fulfilling duties and responsibilities or increasing land targets for construction within their administrative regions. For example, the economically undeveloped Jinyun County launched up to 21 land consolidation projects in 2006 with an investment of up to CNY 0.12 billion, of which 11 projects were completed and accepted, whereby the cultivated land increased by 9866 and 7103 *mu* of the cultivated land were allowed to be used as conversion targets, including 5900 *mu* actually paid for as compensation for Ningbo, Wenzhou, Shaoxing, Jiaojiang, Cixi, Luqiao, etc. at a price of CNY 0.281 billion, more or less a break-even situation if compared with the fiscal revenues of the People's Government of Jinyun County in 2006 (CNY 0.285 billion). For economically underdeveloped areas, the significance of targets selling even went beyond land consolidation to some extent; while for relatively developed areas, the price seemed unworthy mentioning when compared with land targets for construction. This was even more obvious after the policy of linking the increase of urban construction land and decrease of rural residential land was introduced. Frankly, the logic in financing based on no matter land consolidation or market transactions of targets was, similar to that in land finance, to obtain revenues from land (or land targets) selling as a support of the construction of urban (or rural) infrastructure in the region in chorus with the historical background characterized by land-based development.

Indeed, the so-called "Zhejiang paradigm" has been unceasingly questioned and criticized for: (a) evasion of submittal of basic farmland to the central government for approval and fees for paid use of newly added cultivated land, which resulted in the loss of control over total construction land; and (b) relatively poor quality of the cultivated land newly added through consolidation, as compared with the occupied part. The former seemed more notable, for the latter has been always inevitable industrialization and urbanization ever since the introduction of cultivated land protection policies such as balancing occupation and compensation. However, the former was directly related to land administration by the central government and local governments. If dealt with inadequately, it would lead to severe consequences. In particular, the central government must give consideration to how to confine the pilot reform space of local governments with prudence. On December 30, 2007, the General Office of the State Council issued Notice of the General Office of the State Council on Strictly Implementing Laws and Policies concerning Construction Land Owned by the Rural Collective (viz. the No. 71 document issued by the General Office of the State Council of the People's Republic of China in 2007), harshly criticizing "certain local governments in violation of pertinent laws and policies concerning the administration of construction land owned by the rural collective through unauthorized conversion of agricultural land for construction and other issues", which "swept through the nation", and singularly providing that "any experiment or exploration in relation to the land administration system shall not violate the land use control system of the State". Moreover, it also criticized the unauthorized expansion of construction land in the name of circulation of use rights over construction land owned by the rural collective, land consolidation based conversion or linking the increase in land used for urban construction with the decrease in land used for rural construction, and emphasized that "unauthorized expansion of construction land owned by the rural collective and illegal transfer of ownership from the rural collective to the State by means of transformation from village to habitat in various name" should be forbidden. Regarding target conversion, Decree No. 71 stressed that "according to the provisions under the *Regulation on the Implementation of the Land Administration Law of the People's Republic of China*, the area of cultivated land newly added through consolidation shall be only used as compensation targets to compensate for construction, excluding the possibility of being used as construction land targets or to expand construction," thereby completely denying the so-called "Zhejiang paradigm". Since then, compensation with cultivated land newly added through consolidation in Zhejiang and other provinces was suspended.

5.3.1 Summary

On the whole, the central government introduced the policies of urbanization-oriented land replacement and conversion in order to encourage land consolidation (costly as it has been) among local governments, in view of their shortage of interests in this regard as a result of the limited local financial resources ever since 1994 when the tax-sharing system was introduced. In this sense, it can be considered as opening a "tap" in response to the high demand on land from local governments. There is no doubt that the game between the central government and local governments will continue. The central policies introduced over the years have also unveiled the shift of focus from agricultural land to construction land in consolidation along with the increasing shortage of fallback agricultural land resources and the negative consequences on ecology arising from "deforestation-based reclamation", followed by the policy of linking increase of urban construction land and decrease of rural residential land.

5.4 Linking the Increase of Urban Construction Land and the Decrease of Rural Residential Land: A Quota-Stimulated Land Seeking Policy

Compared with opening a "leeway" by conversion targets in land consolidation, this policy most notably differs in "conversion ratio" and the fact that it is geared to the occupation of residential sites owned by the rural collective for construction. More self-evidently, it no longer encourages rural land arrangement in the name of increasing cultivated land, but directly provides compensating land targets for newly added urban construction projects. In sharp contrast with the policy of balancing cultivated land occupation and compensation as characterized by passive regulation, it is embedded with a "target incentive mechanism" that is more positive and more expansionary.

According to the *Resolution on Deepening Reform and Tightening Land Administration* promulgated by the State Council on Oct. 21, 2004, this policy shall "encourage the consolidation of rural land for construction and link increase of urban construction land and decrease of rural residential".

In October 2005, the Ministry of Land and Resources promulgated the *Opinions on Regulating Pilot Work for Linking the Increase in Land Used for Urban Construction with the Decrease in Land Used for Rural Construction* [No. 207 (2005)] in the spirit of the No. 208 document issued by the State Council in 2004, where 8 provinces (or municipalities) were selected for the pilot reform, namely Tianjin, Zhejiang, Jiangsu, Anhui, Shandong, Hubei, Guangdong, and Sichuan. And on January 12, 2006, the *Notice on Including Some Small Cities and Towns in the Regulation of Pilot Work for Linking the Increase in Land Used for Urban Construction with the Decrease in Land Used for Rural Construction* [No. 60 (2006)] was promulgated jointly by the General Office of the State Development and Reform Commission and the General Office of Ministry of Land and Resources, which calls for the included small cities and towns to participate in the pilot reform under the guidance of the local competent departments of development and reform/land and resources in accordance with the requirements provided in No. 207 document issued by the Ministry of Land and Resources in 2005. In 2006, the Ministry of Land and Resources pushed this policy into pilot exploration in Tianjin and other four provinces (or municipalities) in line with the principle of staged reporting and small-scale progressive evolution. As a result, 183 projects were launched, whereby 73,800 *mu* of cultivated land may be used as circulating targets. In April 2007, the participants in a pilot working forum in Chengdu provided a comprehensive analysis and summary of the experience and issues of the pilot work and, on this basis, raised requirements for the future work. According to the *Notice on Further Regulating the Pilot Work for Linking the Increase of Urban Construction Land and Rural Residential Land* [No. 169 (2007)] promulgated by the Ministry of Land and Resources as of July 13, 2007, Inner Mongolia and Henan shall also be included in the pilot work (in all, 10 provinces/autonomous regions/municipalities were included), and it is required to provide strengthened planning and guidance for the pilot work, put the projects under overall examination for approval, tighten up circulating targets supervision, and safeguard the rights and interests of farmers, among other issues.

The implications and key points in the execution of this policy are provided in *the Measures for the Administration of the Trial Work of Linking the Increase in Land Used for Urban Construction with the Decrease in Land Used for Rural Construction* promulgated by the Ministry of Land and Resources on June 27, 2008. According to the operation mechanism, it refers to "the activities of putting together several land blocks of land used for rural construction that are to be cleared up and reclaimed as arable land (land blocks where old buildings shall be dismantled), the land blocks to be used for urban construction (land blocks where new buildings shall be built) and other areas on the basis of the overall land use planning to compose a project area of dismantling old buildings and building new ones (hereinafter referred to as the "project area"), to finally achieve the objective of increasing the effective area of arable land, improving the quality of arable land, economically and intensively using the construction land, and implementing a more reasonable layout of the urban and rural land use through such measures as dismantling old buildings and building new ones, land clear-up and reclamation, and on the basis of ensuring the balance of areas of all kinds of land in the project area". A comparative analysis will reveal its similarity to the policy of land target replacement for construction in nature and expression, which reflects the continuity and exploration of policies introduced in the reform. In Reply No. 138, pilot projects included in the second stage are disclosed, involving a total of 10,246 ha or 153,680 *mu* of land, and the project areas are provided as alternatives. In the *Reply of the Ministry of Land and Resources on Circulating Targets for Linking the Increase of Land Used for Urban Construction and the Decrease in Land Used for Rural Construction in the First Stage* (No. 299 Letter sent by the Ministry of Land and Resources in 2009) in 2009 on March 5, 2009, circulating targets as considerable as 152,750 *mu* (or 10,183.3 ha) were provided to 13 provinces/autonomous regions, namely, Hebei, Inner Mongolia, Liaoning, Jilin, Heilongjiang, Fujian, Jiangxi, Henan, Hunan, Guangdong, Guangxi, Yunnan, and Ningxia. At the 15th Working Meeting of Ministers held by Jiang Daming, the Minister and Secretary of the Leading Party Group of Land and Resources and Chief Inspector of State Land in the afternoon of October 23, 2013, the Ministry of Land and Resources, the *Target Decomposition and Allocation Scheme for Linking the Increase in Land Used for Urban Construction and the Decrease in Land Used for Rural Construction in 2013* was submitted and approved, involving a total of 29 provinces and 0.9 million *mu* of land (Fig. 5.2).

Regarding the logic of this policy, balance of targets is the core of the increase and decrease-linking policy, which means the land originally used for rural construction that are to be cleared up and reclaimed as arable land shall be equal to that used for urban construction under the strict project allocation and approval system. Specifically, (a) dismantle the residencies of farmers in a number of land blocks (i.e., the original homestead of farmers) for reclamation so as to obtain a certain area of cultivated land; (b) select a land block in the project area for the construction of residencies for the farmers (mostly storied buildings); and (c) according to the design logic of the increase and decrease-linking policy, the surplus land (i.e., the area of reclaimed cultivated land minus the area of land used for residential construction for the farmers) may be used as circulating targets to compensate for land blocks used for urban construction in the project area. Target calculation formula: Circulating Target under the policy = Total area of land blocks where old buildings shall be dismantled—Area of the land block used for residential construction for the farmers = Area of land available for urban construction in the project area. The so-called "circulating target" in essence corresponds to a target "pre-borrow" or

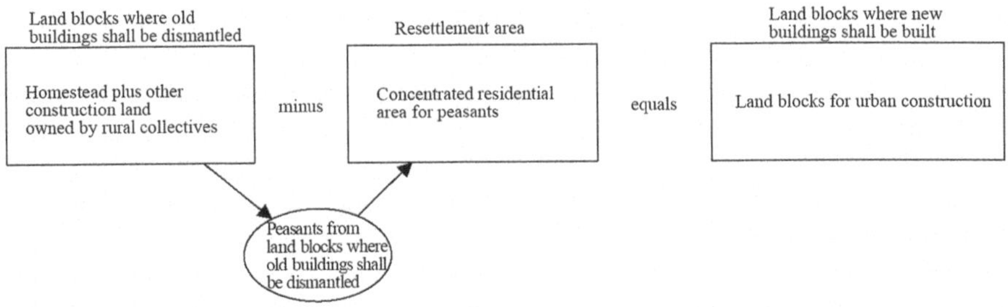

Fig. 5.2 Schematic illustration of the increase and decrease-linking policy

拆旧区：Land blocks where old buildings shall be dismantled

农民的宅基地其他农村集体建设用地：Homestead plus other construction land owned by rural collectives

减去：minus

安置区：Resettlement area

农民集中居住小区：Concentrated residential area for peasants

等于：equals

建新区：Land blocks where new buildings shall be built

城镇建新地块（指标落地地块）：Land blocks for urban construction

拆旧区农民：Peasants from land blocks where old buildings shall be dismantled

"overdraft" system. According to the requirements of this policy, dismantlement and construction can be carried out simultaneously, rather than in tandem, because the dismantlement and reclamation would involve huge volume of works that can be hardly completed in a short term. And in such a context the concept of target "circulating", usually in a cycle of three years, was proposed.

In summary, the main points of the design logic of this policy include: (a) There is a great potential to be exploited in view of the serious waste of land resources used for rural collective construction, in contrast to our call for intensive and effective utilization of land; (b) From the dismantlement and reclamation of land used for rural collective construction, not only an increase of cultivated land but also new residencies for the farmers within the project area may be obtained. Thus, according to the logic of "reverse" balance of cultivated land occupation and compensation, the surplus land may be used for urban construction. In such a way, both the land required for urbanization and improved living conditions of farmers are guaranteed, which is a precondition for building new countryside and nursing countryside by cities on the premise of maintaining 1.8 billion *mu* of cultivated land; (c) This policy shall be implemented in accordance with the closed-loop project scheme characterized by the one-to-one correspondence between blocks subject to dismantlement and those for urban construction as well as the local planning and design, so as to effectively avoid large-scale dismantlement and construction and other disorderly behaviors; and (d) It shall include a strict project examination and approval system, whereby the examination and approval authority shall be held exclusively by the central government, and the pilot work should be submitted to the Ministry of Land and Resources for approval so as to avoid any unauthorized behaviors. Considering the limited approvals for "project targets", the central government shall retain authority on land issues over local governments.

The increase and decrease-linking policy is internally oriented toward extra-budgetary target incentives. How did it make local governments so actively participate in this time-consuming campaign? The fundamental significance of this policy lies in the fact that it has found a new source of targets that is independent from the control system for annual land targets newly added for construction and thus provided ever-increasing "off-plan" land resources for urbanization that would not take up planned targets, as illustrated in Fig. 5.3. For example, in 2012, it was determined that only 450 *mu* of land could be used for urban construction in Feicheng City, Shandong Province, but the actually approved construction projects involved 2500 *mu* of land, because there were two other channels to make up the deficient 2050 *mu* of land: (a) land targets for national or provincial construction projects; and (b) projects where the policy of linking the increase in land used for urban construction and the decrease in land used for rural construction was applicable, which involved 1500 *mu* of land,

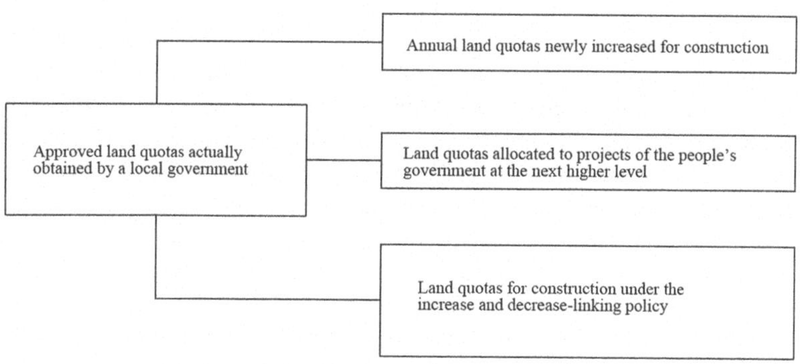

Fig. 5.3 Allocation of construction land targets to local governments

本级政府实际获得审批用地指标: Approved land quotas actually obtained by a local government

本级政府年度新增建设用地指标: Annual land quotas newly increased for construction

上级政府项目自带的用地指标: Land quotas allocated to projects of the people's government at the next higher level

本级政府在增减挂钩政策框架下所得建新区用地指标: Land quotas for construction under the increase and decrease-linking policy

accounting for 60% of the total. In the trinity of land, finance, and fiscal revenues, these extra-budgetary targets have greatly stimulated local governments and, to some extent, opened a tap under the high centralized system. For local governments, this policy has not only helped to complete the respective political tasks while maintaining the existing volume of cultivated land, but even provided a great motivation for comprehensive land consolidation.

A review of the propaganda of this policy reveals that this policy has been promoted as a "political achievement" due to its political correctness which, under the existing bureaucratic system, is actually a result of "official" commonsense. The following is an excerpt representative of the propaganda model from China Land and Resources News, Nov. 23, 2012: "The Bureau of Land and Resources of Funan County, Anhui Province has recently made best of the fine days by accelerating the reclamation in land blocks included in the pilot implementation of the increase and decrease-linking policy within 40 project areas in altogether 13 villages and towns, including Zhonggang, Xincun, Huilong, Tianji, etc. Most of the projects have been progressing smoothly. According to the design requirements, the cultivated land will increase by 143 ha upon the completion of all these projects". Then, what is the relationship between this policy and the protection of cultivated land? Firstly, the design of this policy is not aimed at increasing cultivated land, and as a result of the closed-loop operation, the reclaimed land would be used as circulating targets for urban construction. Therefore, from the perspective of the overall project, there would be no increase in the total area of cultivated land. Moreover, the cultivated land occupied for urban construction shall anyway be compensated for in order to achieve balance. In this sense, this policy is just an approach to balancing the occupation and compensation of cultivated land. Secondly, local governments involved in the pilot projects, especially those governing the land blocks where old buildings shall be dismantled, will mostly prefer to either sell or use the target to compensate for land used for construction within the respective areas under their jurisdiction, rather than retain it as "added cultivated land", considering that the costs far exceeds proceeds. As indicated by the statistical data on a pilot project in Wushan Township, Dayi County, Chengdu City, Sichuan Province in Table 5.2, the cultivated land in land blocks subject to dismantlement increased by 547.86 *mu*, the resettlement residential area occupied 23.66 *mu*, and land used for urban construction totaled 523.20 *mu*. So the area of newly added effective cultivated land was only 0.9 *mu*. The results of other pilot projects have been mostly the same, for a perfect balance between targets and capital is the first principle for project propaganda. Thus, it is obvious that from the perspective of either inherent spirit or results, this policy will not lead to any increase in the total cultivated land which, at best, will not be decreased anyway. Of course, this is a great "political achievement" under the current political framework, even though what degree the "retained cultivated land" will safeguard food security and promote agriculture modernization is highly contentious. Of course, this issue will not be scrutinized.

From the target calculation formula, it can be seen that land available for urban construction on the rightmost is what local governments are in urgent need of. And the left side of the equation indicates that given the dismantlement scale as

Table 5.2 Targets balance sheet for the project linking the increase in land used for urban construction and the decrease in land used for rural construction in Wushan Township, Dayi County, Chengdu City, Sichuan Province

		Block	Area		Remaining or used target	Increased cultivated land		
Land block where old buildings shall be dismantled		Xiakou village and Lianghekou community, Wushan Township	547.86 *mu*, originally used for rural collective construction		Remaining target: 547.86 *mu*	547.86 *mu*		0.9 *mu* in total
Land blocks where new buildings shall be built	Land blocks for urban construction	Longfeng community, Qingxia town	540.37 *mu*	523.20 *mu*, agricultural land	Used target: 523.20 *mu*	−523.30 *mu*	−546.96 *mu* in total	
				17.17 *mu*, land used for construction				
	Resettlement residential area	Daping village, Wushan township	23.66 *mu*, occupied agricultural land		Used target: 23.66 *mu*	−23.66 *mu*		

determined by the people's government at a higher level, local governments shall base their maximization of land available for urban construction on the minimization of the resettlement residential area, which would lead to a one-sided pursuit of linking targets, which has been be fulfilled by, on the one hand, arranging multi-storied resettlement housing, enhancing the volume fraction, and thus reducing the area of land required for resettlement as possible, on the other hand, ignoring the overall plan for land utilization and related special plans, exclusively selecting such villages and industrial/mining areas as relatively large in floor area per household and even, in some regions, going beyond the allocated target so as to accommodate urban construction. Therefore, in many regions, the local governments have drawn a "baseline" to determine who might be included in the project, which means there is actually a lower limit for the surplus land available for construction. This is a result of alienation in execution. Generally speaking, there has been a burning desire to break the various land control policies among local governments, for example, by this "leeway-leaving" policy.

5.4.1 Summary

The "project-oriented" increase and decrease-linking policy is designed to find out an emergency solution to the shortage of land for local governments. It has provided an effective target incentive mechanism and, in the implementation process, gradually become a major source of land available for construction. However, it has been accompanied by the following risks. Firstly, the central government has been at risk of losing control over local governments in this regard. Under the trinity development mode, local governments ventured large-scale off-project operations, while it has become increasingly difficult for the central government to achieve effective control over local governments as a result of the confinement in their relationship. For example, prior to the nationwide inspection in 2011, Hebei Province was only allocated 12,000 *mu* as linking targets the Ministry of Land and Resources, but it in fact obtained extra targets for construction as notable as over 0.5 million *mu* through the transformation of 7500 villages within 3 years. Anhui and Inner Mongolia even steered clear of the pilot work by independently promulgating provisional measures for construction-motivated land replacement. On the one hand, the central government focused on the investigation of "unlawful practices"; on the other hand, in hope of maintaining the enthusiasm and vitality of local governments in development, it had to expand the scope and scale of pilot projects. In this sense, the local pilot projects have been obviously characterized by fixed interests. Secondly, it might entail the in-flow of substantive social capital. This policy has been promoted under the project scheme that is essentially a new resource redistribution mechanism most notably characterized by the downward capital transfer, which must be supported by local governments at all levels with relevant policies and funds (otherwise, it would be at risk of losing the project). However, raising supporting funds has been uneasy for local governments.

Meanwhile, land selling-based fiscal revenues have also been unsustainable for local governments, and we have been faced with a huge financial pressure in nurturing the countryside and building new villages. Therefore, local governments have been difficult to come up with necessary capital for the rural areas. Under such a background, the in-flow of rational and profit-driven social capital became inevitable. How would the involvement of substantive capital influence the local governance ecology remains an open question. Thirdly, we should also be aware of the risks with the society and local governance accompanying the large-scale resettlement in concentrated communities. Land-deprived farmers would witness a sharp increase in living costs after they move into the concentrated communities. Thus, the previous economical lifestyle could be hardly maintained, coupled with their high possibility of unemployment, would inevitably lead to social instability to some extent. In addition, the inadequate self-government of the original village communities and mixed habitation would also cause a centrifugal force to be reckoned with, adding to the pressure on social management at the grassroots level. As villagers and even the grass-roots society became more and more dependent on local governments, the "floating regime" has been gradually transformed into a "nursing government". Faced with the ever-increasing pressure and risks with local governance, the inexperienced local governments still need to multiple their efforts so as to usher in a new epoch.

5.5 Introduction of Plan Management and Liquidation Inspection: Narrowing Down the "Leeway"

The increase and decrease-linking policy has considerably enhanced the motivation of local governments for land consolidation. From the standpoint of the relationship between the central government and local governments, the latter's interpretation of policies promulgated by the former shall be given due considerations at the outset of designing, and even deemed as an integral part of such policies. For example, under the increase and decrease-linking policy has enticed local governments to challenge unauthorized expansion of pilot projects, and more importantly, gave them an "excuse" for such behaviors. Some projects excluded from pilot reform were executed in the name of balancing urban and rural development and building a new countryside. Noting this phenomenon, Chen Xiwen criticized that "it is not rare to use up the cultivated land newly increased from village merging for urban construction, which will not only lead to an unauthorized expansion of the urban construction, but also entice local governments to rake in enormous land revenues from the price difference between urban and rural land for construction, and consequently, this phenomenon has been more and more wide-spread, bringing about an unprecedented campaign characterized by rural dismantlement and urban construction. Therefore, Notice of the General Office of State Council on Strictly Implementing Laws and Regulations concerning Rural Collective Land for Construction (viz. the No. 71 docuemnt issued by the General Office of the State

Council of the People's Republic of China in 2007) was promulgated on Dec. 30, 2007, stressing that "the pilot projects linking the increase in land used for urban construction and the decrease in land used for rural construction shall be strictly controlled within the designated scope in line with the overall plan for land utilization and the requirements for urban/township/village planning, so as to ensure sustainable increase in the total volume of land used for urban and rural construction while maintaining the total area of cultivated and agricultural land at a steady level; and large-scale dismantlement/construction contrary to the wishes of farmers, forced relocation or infringement on the interests of farmers in the name of pilot reform shall be forbidden".

The Decision of the CCCPC on Several Major Issues Concerning Promoting the Development of Rural Reform was adopted at the Third Plenary Session of the 17th Central Committee of the Communist Party of China on Oct. 12, 2008, stressing that "land newly increased from consolidation of rural residential sites and villages shall be foremost reclaimed; any use as compensation for construction shall be consistent with the general plan for land utilization and included in the annual land plan for construction, whereby priority shall be given to collective construction projects". And according to the *Notice on the National Plan for Land Utilization (draft) of 2009* (viz. the No. 9 document issued by the Ministry of Land and Resources in 2009) issued by the Ministry of Land and Resources on 10 Feb., 2009, "all land involved in use transformation, such as those subject to the increase and decrease-linking policy, rural construction, development of unutilized land, reclamation from the sea, etc., shall be included in the annual plan for unified management.

Acting in the spirit of the *Notice of the State Council on Strictly Regulating the Pilots Work for Linking the Increase in Land Used for Urban Construction and the Decrease in Land Used for Rural Construction and Effectively Carrying out Land Consolidation in Rural Areas* (viz. the No. 47 document issued by the State Council in 2010), *Working Program for Pilot Projects Linking the Increase in Land Used for Urban Construction and the Decrease in Land Used for Rural Construction and Inspection of Land Consolidation in Rural Areas* was promulgated jointly by the Ministry of Land and Resources, Office of the Central Rural Work Leading Group, National Development and Reform Commission, Ministry of Finance, Ministry of Environmental Protection, Ministry of Agriculture, and Ministry of Housing and Urban-Rural Development on Feb. 16, 2011, calling for "comprehensively inspecting the pilot projects, rural land consolidation and unauthorized land replacement for construction under various names since 2006 with the view of finding out all the relevant problems and carrying out serious rectification and regulation correspondingly in accordance with the requirements under the policy, conscientiously summing up relevant working experiences, improving the rules and regulations, strengthening supervision and management, proposing solutions and promoting the reform and innovation on the basis of an in-depth study of the institutional mechanism and other deep-seated issues, and enhancing information construction and "one-map" dynamic regulation of land and resources so as to ensure the regulated, healthy and orderly progression of the pilot projects and land consolidation in rural areas". On June 19, 2011, the Ministry of Land and Resources promulgated the *Opinions on Some Issues Concerning the Pilot Work for Linking the Increase in Land Used for Urban Construction and the Decrease in Land Used for Rural Construction and Land Consolidation in Rural Areas*, offering specific suggestions on the treatment of unauthorized expansion of pilot projects, off-target operations, unregulated management, delayed reclamation, etc. and, regarding the concrete treatments of the problems with land consolidation in rural areas, stressing that "such transfer of land targets for rural construction to urban areas as involved in consolidation and replacement of land for rural construction shall be fully rectified by the end of Aug. 2011, so that those included in regulated management in line with the requirements for the project area shall be submitted to the Ministry of Land and Resources for approval and thereafter enter both the legend and stock, subject to treatments for off-target pilot projects by deducting the omitted part from the annual circulating targets, while those excluded from regulated management shall be subject to withdrawal of the approval for land replacement, suspension of the said land targets for construction, and deduction from the annual planned targets of land newly added for construction based on the occupied area. In addition, the *Notice of the Ministry of Land and Resources on Strictly Regulating the Pilot Work for Linking the Increase in Land Used for Urban Construction and the Decrease in Land Used for Rural Construction* (viz. the No. 224 document issued by the Ministry of Land and Resources in 2011) promulgated as of Nov. 26, 2011 not only stressed to fully recognize the significance of the pilot work by urging competent departments to "attach great importance to and provide active propaganda and proper guidance on this issue in an attempt to creating a positive social environment to safeguard and promote the pilot work", but also called on the people's government in all provincial units to strictly regulate the pilot work by insisting on project management and closed operations, whereby "forced dismantlement, construction or resettlement in multi-storied buildings contrary to the will of collective organizations and farmers shall be forbidden, and any cross-county project area shall not be approved". All these provisions indicate that this policy (adopted in 2004) has entered the inspection stage. However, it is not accurate to refer it as a "stage", because this policy has released tremendous energy that can be hardly curbed by a document, despite of the numerous difficulties in obtaining approval for pilot projects.

It is also stressed in No. 1 Document issued by the central government in 2013 to "reform and improve the rural homestead system, strengthen management, safeguard the land use rights of farmers, promote the comprehensive rural land consolidation according to law, strictly regulate the pilot work for linking the increase in land used for urban construction and the decrease in land used for rural construction as well as the transfer of collective-owned land for commercial construction, and bar out the rural collective-owned land used for non-commercial construction from the market" By stipulating to "bar out the rural collective-owned land used for non-commercial construction from the market", on the one hand, it carries on the spirit of the Third Plenary Session of the 17th CCCPC of 2008 in providing that "a unified construction land market covering all urban and rural areas shall be gradually established and, for rural collective-owned land obtained in accordance with law for commercial construction, the land use right shall be transferred in a public and normative manner in such uniformed and tangible land market so that it may enjoy equal rights and interests with state-owned land under the premise of its consistency with planning", turning up the "tap" for the rural collective-owned land to enter the market for commercial construction; on the other hand, the central government shall stand firmly against the marketization of other rural land, and "strict regulation" has been maintained over the increase and decrease-linking policy.

Chapter 6
Local Practice

Closed project operation, as a key component in the design logic of the increase and decrease-linking policy, is characterized by the strict one-to-one correspondence between blocks to be dismantled and those for urban construction. The surplus land targets for construction of the former can be only used within the project package. Any cross-district/county project area shall be forbidden. On June 7, 2007, Chongqing and Chengdu were approved by the State Council as "Pilot Areas for the National Comprehensive Supportive Reform for Balancing Urban and Rural Areas", and thus broadened the horizon for policy exploration. These two cities have made great efforts in exploring market trading of targets and thus achieved high abstract marketization. By "target drift", it means the land targets for construction obtained from reclamation and resettlement may be traded within the specific limits on the land property exchange platform between the land blocks where old buildings shall be dismantled and those where new buildings shall be built, and targets obtained from consolidation in the former may be listed for selling. Therefore, one-to-one correspondence between the two sides becomes unnecessary. It is visualized by local officials as an "enclave". Zhou Qiren et al. considers such a revolutionary move as a typical return of powers to the society and a reform of the land system to "allow farmers share the land revenues increment from urbanization" (Fig. 6.1).

Based on the exploration on market trading of targets in Chengdu and Chongqing, a new double-track project-based system has been established. This system is characterized by the parallelism of target "drift" based on market trading and such pilot work for linking the increase in land used for urban construction and the decrease in land used for rural construction as promoted by the government department of land and resources in a number of provinces and municipalities. In Chongqing, these two tracks refer to land quotas and the increase and decrease-linking policy; and in Chengdu, high and low-level increase and decrease linking policies, respectively. This new double-track system has had significant bearing on the practice orientations of local governments, as well as the relationship among governments at all levels. Both Chongqing's land quota exchange platform

F. Zhou and M. Tan, *Relationship between the Central Government and Local Governments of Contemporary China*, Social Development Experiences in China,
DOI 10.1007/978-981-10-4388-8_6

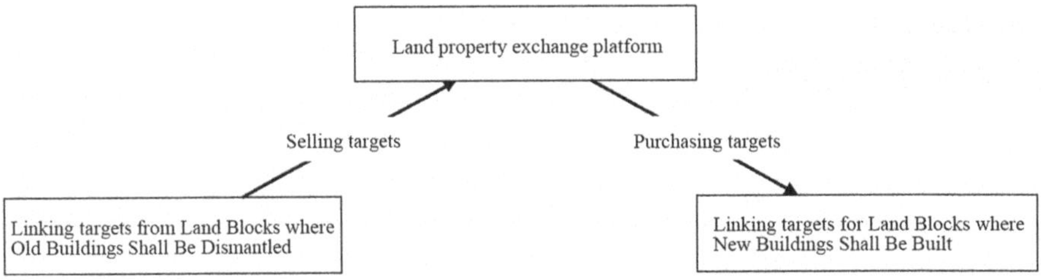

Fig. 6.1 Target drift under the property exchange platform in Chongqing and Chengdu

拆旧区：Land Blocks where Old Buildings Shall be Dismantled

农民的宅基地其他农村集体建设用地：Homestead plus Other Construction Land Owned by Rural Collectives

减去：Minus

安置区：Resettlement Area

农民集中居住小区：Concentrated Residential Area for Peasants

等于：Equals

建新区：Land Blocks where New Buildings Shall Be Built

城镇建新地块（指标落地地块）：Land Blocks for Urban Construction

拆旧区农民：Peasants from Land Blocks where Old Buildings Shall Be Dismantled

and Chengdu Agriculture Equity Exchange have made a break-through on the basis of the increase and decrease-linking policy to different degrees, although basically designed within the same framework under the policy.

6.1 Market-Oriented Logic of Quota Drift: A Case Study of the Land Quota System in Chongqing Municipality

The Ministry of Land and Resources signed a strategic cooperation memorandum with Chongqing Municipal People's Government in August 2008, in favor of establishing a rural land exchange in the city so as to explore a new land utilization mechanism and a new cultivated land protection mode. On Oct. 24, 2008, Chongqing Municipal People's Government issued an official document, expressing its agreement on establishing Chongqing Rural Land Exchange. On Dec. 4, the Exchange was formally established and carried out for the first time land quota transactions. Later on Jan. 29, 2009, *Several Opinions of the State Council on Promoting the Balance of Urban and Rural Reform and Development in Chongqing City* was promulgated, explicitly proposing to establish Chongqing

Rural Land Exchange with the view of pilot transactions in kind or targets, thereby endowing Chongqing the right to take a step ahead in the reform.

What does it mean by "land quota"? In accordance with the provisions in Article 18 of the *Interim Measures for the Management of Chongqing Rural Land Exchange*, the land quota that may be traded at Chongqing Rural Land Exchange shall include targets obtained from reclamation of rural homestead and the land for ancillary facilities, township-run enterprises and rural collective construction, such as rural public facilities and utilities, subject to the strict inspection and acceptance by competent departments of land administration". In general, its operation mechanism involves the following 5 steps: (a) Special planning for projects linking the increase in land used for urban construction and the decrease in land used for rural construction: According to the planned scope and layout of projects, this is the basis of "land quota"; (b) Application and reclamation upon approval: Upon reclamation of the rural homestead and the land for ancillary facilities, rural households shall not apply for land use for homestead or ancillary facilities; (c) Acceptance: Upon acceptance, an application shall be filed with the competent administrative department under Chongqing Municipal Bureau of Land and Resources for confirmation and issuance of a document of approval; (d) Exchange and proceeds distribution: The exchange of "land quota" shall be carried out at Chongqing Rural Land Exchange. All legal persons and natural persons with independent civil capacity shall be entitled to the purchase of "land quota" through public bidding, and flat base prices shall be determined for reference, giving due consideration to reclamation costs, fees for paid use of land newly added for construction, and other factors. In accordance with the design of the land quota system, the revenues from the exchange of "land quota", subject to tax payments, shall mostly belong to the rural households, and revenues from the exchange of contractual rights of agricultural and forest land shall all belong to the involved rural households. According to the relevant provisions, 85% of the balance of the price of land quota and costs of reclamation and financing shall be paid to the farmer households who have withdrawn from their homesteads, where the average rate shall be no less than CNY 96,000 per μ; and the remaining 15% shall be delivered to the rural collective economic organization, where the average rate shall be no less than CNY 17,000 per μ; (e) Fulfillment: For developers who have purchased land quota, it does not mean the corresponding volume of land is already available, for the practical significance of land quota shall be only recognized upon fulfillment. Therefore, the bid-winning developer needs to seek for such land blocks as have not been requisitioned by the State yet but conform to the requirements of market development within the framework of urban planning and the general plan for land utilization and, following the nationalization of such land, complete the legal procedures (including bidding, auction, listing, etc.) before taking over the right to use the urban land. In such a way, the land quota is met.

Therefore, there is a possibility for the land quota purchased by the developer to be "frustrated" and thus for the land development project to be suspended. This would necessarily entail economic losses borne by the land quota purchaser. The land quota can be only fulfilled with the support of the local government, thereby providing a rent-seeking space to some extent. In the subsequent reform of the land quota system, Chongqing Municipal People's Government abolished the constraint on the effective term of land quota, which reduced the risks of "frustration" to a certain degree. Anyway, it is improper to expect straight fulfillment of land quota.

The volume of land quota trade in Chongqing since 2008 has reached 111,000 μ at a gross knock-down rate of CNY 22.2 billion. Notably, in 2012, these two figures were 22,300 μ and CNY 4.7 billion, respectively. The average knock-down price ever since 2008 is approximately CNY 200,000/μ, and it is alleged that more than CNY 20 billion has been invested in re-feeding agriculture, countryside and farmers. At the working meeting on land resources and housing management, it was noted by Huang Qifan, the Mayor of Chongqing City, that "land quota has become an integral part of the bonus from the reform of rural constructions in Chongqing". As a mortgage in financing (witnessed in local practices), "land quota" is highly productive even prior to fulfillment. It is publicly reported that CNY 30 million was lent under the gage of land quota estimated at CNY 42.7 million, the first move in Chongqing. As a result of the abolition of the provision that the annual volume of land quota trade shall not exceed 10% of the annual planned land targets by the State Council, the annual volume of land quota trade has been ever-increasing in recent years, reaching around 20% of the annual planned land targets (Table 6.1).

The marketized land quota and newly increased land targets for construction subject to top-down administrative ratification constituted a double-track system. In order to avoid any conflicts arising from the correlation between the planned unpaid targets and the paid targets obtained from "land quota", a series of documents (represented by *Interim Measures for the Management of Chongqing Rural Land Exchange*) were promulgated. According to these documents, planned targets shall be only allocated to industrial/public facilities, education/health sectors and other utilities, and domestic demands-expanding projects, while profit-oriented land shall be excluded, for which only land quota shall be applicable. However, the original planned allocation method shall be maintained in counties/districts from the outer

Table 6.1 Planning and utilization of the three categories of land targets for construction in Chongqing (2008–2011). *Unit* μ

Year	Planned targets allocated by the State		Targets under the increase and decrease-linking policy	Land quota		
	Planned	Utilized		Traded	Fulfilled	Portion to targets allocated by the State (%)
2008	137,600	133,300	4700	1100	0	0.80
2009	138,700	118,700	15,000	12,400	900	8.94
2010	150,400	127,400	10,000	22,200	5900	14.77
2011	164,900	154,700	30,000	52,900	26,400	32.08

suburbs. This new land classification mechanism or double-track target distribution system was not established under the market principle. The provision that only land quota shall be applicable for profit-oriented land indicates that for developers, the development costs of a certain land block in the city would increase by the portion arising from land quota, namely the costs of dismantlement and reclamation in land blocks where old buildings shall be dismantled plus those of construction in the resettlement residential area.

6.2 Relationship Among Local Governments at Various Levels Under the Land Quota System

In simple terms, the "supplier" and "buyer" are designed under the land quota system. It can be seen from the foregoing analysis that land quotas, (subject to circulation and drift) have a direct impact on the regional development potential. If the local fiscal revenues are not dominated by those from targets, local governments would universally pursue the "fulfillment of targets within their respective region". The uneven development and administration may be visualized from where land quota is fulfilled. Statistics show that as of March 2012, the land quota fulfilled in Chongqing claims a total of 21,300 μ, including 17,700 μ in the main urban zone (accounting for 83%), 3000 μ in the 6 regional hubs (accounting for 14%) and 600 μ in other districts or counties (accounting for only 3%). All these cast a light on the subtle relationship among local governments at various levels. In general, the main urban zone outperformed the districts and counties located in outer suburbs, and thus had priority in the allotment of land targets. In fact, most targets have been fulfilled in the main urban zone ever since the adoption of the land quota system.

Therefore, for land quota suppliers, the compensation can hardly accommodate the requirements for local development. And local governments have become more and more aware of the significance of such "right to develop". So, how shall we mobilize land quota suppliers? In recent years, the competent department of land and resources in Chongqing have assigned annual land quota supply targets to each district/county, and included such targets in the assessment indicators of government work, arousing severe dissatisfaction among the people's governments at the county/township level. According to an investigation of Jiangjin District, Chongqing City—the cradle of land quota (by Zhong Yang 2012), after numerous land targets for construction were re-distributed to other areas in 2008 and 2009, Jiangjin District had not been favored by any extra-preferential policy for its contribution; instead, it was even faced with a shortage of land necessary for its own development. While it failed to obtain other land targets for construction, the unique solution had to be a purchase of land quota at the land exchange. However, the price had risen from CNY 80,000 to 200,000/μ, which was undoubtedly somewhat unacceptable. "In view of this situation, some people's governments at the district/county level became no longer willing to undertake the supply of newly added land targets for construction for exchange, and shifted their focus to the more favorable projects linking the increase in land used for urban construction and the decrease in land used for rural construction". The so-called "more favorable projects linking the increase in land used for urban construction and the decrease in land used for rural construction" shall be only recognized in the standard sense, characterized by the one-to-one correspondence between land blocks where old buildings shall be dismantled and those for urban construction, with the view of retaining circulating targets for internal use in entirety, unlike those listed in the land quota trading market for exchange and drifting.

In order to arouse the enthusiasm of people's governments at the district/county level in their supply of land quota and curb their ardor for involvement in the "regulated" increase and decrease-linking policy, the *Urgent Circular on Steadily Implementing the Pilot Work for Linking the Increase in Land Used for Urban Construction and the Decrease in Land Used for Rural Construction* (viz. The No. 127 document issued by the Bureau of Land, Resources and Housing Administration of Chongqing Municipality in 2011) promulgated by Chongqing Municipal People's Government in 2011 imposes constraints on the admittance of pilot projects. It is provided that "the buildings on the homestead and land for affiliated facilities of farmers shall no longer be dismantled as the case was in pilot projects, nor new buildings built on the profit-oriented land in the main urban zone where the people's government at the district/county level is located", and "the said projects shall be only approved for public welfare and utilities". All these indicate that the demands for local development can no longer be satisfied through "regulated" projects under the increase and decrease-linking policy. This has been especially attractive for: (a) plenty of circulating targets may be available through dismantlement and reclamation on the homestead of farmers; and (b) circulating targets for profit-oriented land in the city may be fulfilled, which will promote the regional urbanization and increase fiscal revenues from land. In view of these two advantages, Circular No. 127 proposes efficient counter-measures and thus has effectively curbed the ardor of local governments for involvement of this policy.

On the other hand, the Chongqing Municipal People's Government played "carrot and stick". In order to alleviate the discontent of people's governments at the district/county level, Chongqing Municipal Bureau of Land Resources and Housing Management issued the *Notice on Conscientiously Doing a Good Job on the Reclamation of Rural Land for Construction* in October 2011. It is provided that for any district and/or county as a land quota supplier, land targets newly added for construction equivalent to 30% of its actual land quota trade volume shall be allotted as a bonus for urban construction and infrastructure projects, so as to enhance their ardor for the supply of land quota. On the whole, the main urban zone is still relatively advantageous as a result of the existing administrative system. On the other hand, based on the development trend, the people's governments at the district/county level will become inevitably less and less interested in offering land quota.

6.3 From Admittance Ratification to Utilization Ratification: A Case Study of the Equity Exchange Platform in Rural Areas of Chengdu, Sichuan Province

On June 7, 2007, Chengdu and Chongqing were approved as "Pilot Areas for the National Comprehensive Supportive Reform for Balancing Urban and Rural Areas", allowing exploration on the reform of rural land management policies. The reconstruction, new countryside building and other urban projects re-feeding the countryside immediately following the Wenchuan earthquake in 2008 laid a heavy burden on the Chengdu Municipal People's Government. Without extra funding granted by the central government, this could be hardly addressed solely by the re-feeding strategy. According to a senior official from Chengdu, the urbanization of half of the 6 million of rural population would require an investment of about CNY 600 billion; but the total fiscal revenues were merely slightly more than CNY 70 billion in 2007, despite of a notable increase over the previous year. "So, who can afford this undertaking?" Therefore, it was urgent to introduce new approaches to land financing necessary for rural construction and post-earthquake recovery. In order to alleviate the development pressure as well as difficulties in post-earthquake reconstruction, the Ministry of Land and Resources provided preferential terms with respect to the increase and decrease-linking policy, including inter-county land transfer and the use of proceeds from targets trade for the construction of new residencies. The former allowed the local government to maximize land revenues under this policy, vesting residential structures newly built with social capital on the homestead of farmers with perfect title, which means such structures may be allowed into the market for exchange and huge sums of social capital would be attracted, while the latter spared the necessity of completing the entire cycle that involves dismantlement, construction, acceptance and other procedures, and thus facilitated the financing for comprehensive land consolidation and resettlement residential projects, as a means of racing against time for post-earthquake reconstruction. The effective term of these preferential policies was three years. Upon expiration, the Chengdu Municipal People's Government filed an application with the central government for laying it down in the form of a basic policy (Fig. 6.2).

Under such a background, Chengdu Agriculture Equity Exchange was established on Oct. 13, 2008 and has ever since been providing the following three categories of services: (a) exchange of rural property rights, including rural land contractual management right, forestry property, rural housing ownership, use right of collective-owned construction land, equity of rural economic collectives, etc.; (b) exchange of targets for balancing occupation and compensation as well as those for linking the increase in land used for urban construction and the decrease in land used for rural collective construction as obtained from comprehensive land consolidation; and (c) disposal of assets. The exchange of targets, as included in the second category, is the same in nature with the land quota system implemented in Chongqing. Specifically, the transferor of the use right of collective-owned

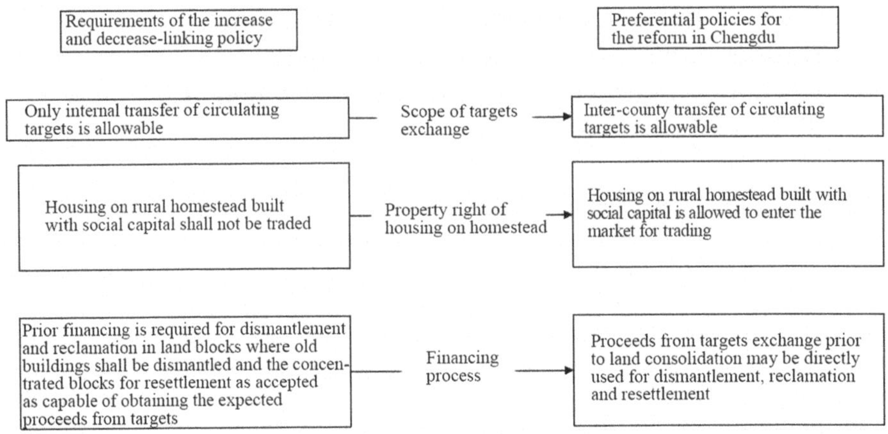

Fig. 6.2 Comparison of the requirements of the increase and decrease-linking policy and preferential policies for reform in Chengdu

增减挂钩政策要求：Requirements of the increase and decrease-linking policy

周转指标的县域内流转：Only internal transfer of circulating targets is allowable

社会资金在农民宅基地建房不可交易：Housing on rural homestead built with social capital shall not be traded

拆旧区拆旧复垦、安置农民集中居住经验收可获得指标收入、需要前期融资：Prior financing is required for dismantlement and reclamation in land blocks where old buildings shall be dismantled and the concentrated blocks for resettlement as accepted as capable of obtaining the expected proceeds from targets

指标交易范围：Scope of targets exchange

宅基地房屋产权：Property right of housing on homestead

融资流程：Financing process

成都改革优惠政策：Preferential policies for the reform in Chengdu

周转指标的跨县域流转：Inter-county transfer of circulating targets is allowable

社会资金在农民宅基地建房具有大产权、可入市交易：Housing on rural homestead built with social capital is allowed to enter the market for trading

土地整理前提前获得指标交易收入直接用于拆旧区拆旧复垦与安置农民：Proceeds from targets exchange prior to land consolidation may be directly used for dismantlement, reclamation and resettlement construction land must be an economic collective, and the use right of collective-owned construction land used by economic collectives may be only transferred on the strength of consent by more than 2/3 of the members or villager representatives expressed at the villagers' meeting. In such a way, the restrictions under existing legal provisions may be effectively evaded, because it is a legal rule that rural land shall be owned by collectives, and individual farmers shall not be entitled to direct transfer of such land. In the practices in Chengdu, the economic collectives, as the transferor, successfully avoided basic legal risks.

The first auction of land targets at the Chengdu Agriculture Equity Exchange under the policy of linking the increase in land used for urban construction and the decrease in land used for rural construction was held in December 2010. Since then, admittance ratification has been gradually replaced by utilization ratification as a trading rule, mirroring the attitude and considerations of both local governments and the central government in the land reform. This subsection will make an analysis on the modifications of trading rules.

Admittance ratification: targets have become the precondition of land purchase.

Let's begin with an excerpt from the *Notice on Implementing the Admittance Ratification System for the Transfer of Use Rights of state-owned Profit-Oriented Construction Land* promulgated by the Chengdu Municipal Bureau of Land and Resources on Aug. 5, 2010: "In order to arouse the enthusiasm of farmer collectives/households and social capital in participating in the comprehensive consolidation of rural land and building a long-term mechanism for re-feeding the countryside and balancing the development of urban and rural areas, and according to the relevant provisions under the *Circular of Chengdu Municipal People's Government on Forwarding the Opinions of Chengdu Land and Resources Bureau and Other Departments on Improving the Land Transaction System to Promote Comprehensive Consolidation of Rural Land and Rural Housing Construction* (*Trial*) (viz. the No. 59 document issued by the Office of the People's Government of Chengdu in 2010), matters related to admittance ratification for the transfer of use rights of state-owned profit-oriented construction land are hereby notified as follows". According to the definition provided therein, "whoever wishes to participate in such bidding of use rights of state-owned construction land as announced after Aug. 1, 2010 in Chengdu and has filed an application shall sign up for bidding on the strength of a construction land target certificate for the corresponding area or a receipt of due security for such land target for construction". This is a precondition for bidding the use right of state-owned construction land. In other words, only holders of construction land target certificates are allowed for bidding. So, how can we obtain such a certificate? In accordance with the provisions therein, "bidders can procure land targets for construction directly from the comprehensive consolidation of rural land or buy such targets for the corresponding area of land and obtain a receipt on the strength of security payment at the Chengdu Agriculture Equity Exchange". By comparison, we can see that among these three approaches to target procurement, namely (a) comprehensive consolidation of rural land, (b) purchase at the Chengdu Agriculture Equity Exchange, and (c) security payment, bidders usually select (b) and/or (c), because the comprehensive consolidation in rural areas usually involves a long project term, complicated works, and high risks that are especially unfavorable for most enterprises. In contrast, it would be much easier by purchase or security payment. Obviously, these considerations are inconsistent with the original intention of the system design of "mobilizing the entire society to participate in rural land remediation".

Consequently, the *Circular on Further Improving the Admittance Ratification System for the Transfer of Use Right of state-owned Land for Profit-Oriented Construction* was promulgated by the Chengdu Bureau of Land and Resources on Nov. 16, 2010. It is provided that "in order to fully arouse the enthusiasm of farmer collectives/households and social capital in participating in the consolidation of rural land and building a long-term mechanism for re-feeding the countryside and balancing the development of urban and rural areas, the admittance ratification system for the transfer of use rights of state-owned land for profit-oriented construction shall be further improved, and related matters are hereby notified as follows … whoever wishes to participate in the bidding of use rights of state-owned land for profit-oriented construction as announced after Jan. 1, 2011 in Chengdu and has filed an application shall sign up for bidding on the strength of a construction land target certificate for the corresponding area, and the original provision for signing up by a receipt of due security for such land target for construction shall be no longer applicable". Most notably, this is actually a denial of the third approach to obtaining the target certificate provided in the Circular of 5 Aug., 2010. Since then, the certificate can be only obtained through either comprehensive consolidation of rural land or exchange at the Chengdu Agriculture Equity Exchange.

Since then, "targets" have become the precondition for land developers to enter the primary land market and to purchase the use right of state-owned land for profit-oriented construction in Chengdu. Whoever wishes to launch such a construction project shall first either complete comprehensive consolidation of rural land or buy the necessary land targets on the exchange platform. There is usually a lack of interests in capital investment in rural land consolidation. So there remains a single straight approach to this end, i.e., by buying the necessary targets. According to the provisions on "admittance ratification", it is impossible to enjoy the use right of state-owned land for construction without the so-called "target certificate". In a sense, buying such "target certificate" has been a rehearsal or an integral part of the procurement of use right of state-owned land for profit-oriented construction. Highly sensitive to policy changes as it may be, capital usually makes exaggerated reactions to some extent, based on the expectations and judgment of the policy. Without targets, any government would be unable to continue to involve themselves in the bidding process. Thus, it would be difficult for them to complete land reserves, leading to a break-off of the complicated real estate chain. Therefore, there was naturally a firestorm in the first targets auction in Chengdu.

The *Circular of Chengdu Agriculture Equity Exchange on Trade of Land Targets for Construction* (viz. the No. 004 document issued by Chengdu Agriculture Equity Exchange on the quotas for transaction in 2010) was promulgated on 3 Dec., 2010. And immediately, 2000 μ of land for construction was listed for bidding on Dec. 17, 2010. It was provided that the listed land targets for construction could be admitted for bidding of the use right of state-owned land for profit-oriented construction (industrial land exclusive) in Chengdu (including the main urban zone and districts/municipalities/counties within the second and third rings). The auction was based on live and open outcry as well as the principle of the highest bidder, and the starting price was CMY 150,000/μ. Under the design of admittance ratification, land targets for construction have become scarce commodities and rage at the market. More than 100 developers participated in the auction. The highest and average prices were CNY 920,000/μ and 720,000/μ, respectively, and the turnover totaled CNY 1457.8 million, approximately 1/3 of those witnessed in the land auction as of May 9, 2010. Thus, the premium rate was as high as 385.93%. Specifically, Poly won the bid of 2 land quotas (for 100 μ each) as Bidder 141 at CNY 700,000/μ and CNY 690,000 million/μ, respectively, plus another one for 200 μ from Tenderee 16 as Bidder 145 at CNY 660,000/μ. Thus, the total transactions amounted CNY 271,000,000. Rise Sun, as Bidder 47, procured 4 land quotas with a total of CNY 135,700,000, each for 10, 20, 50 and 100 μ at CNY 780,000/μ, CNY 820,000/μ, CNY 850,000/μ and CNY 690,000/μ respectively. Gemdale was the bid winner of a land quota for 200 μ at the unit price of CNY 680,000/μ as Bidder 144, and the total payment was CNY 136,000. In addition, although non-engaged in the real estate sector, CNPC also concluded a deal amounting CNY 16,800,000 in total for 20 μ at a unit price of CNY 840,000/μ as Bidder 1 (Table 6.2).

The first target auction achieved even better results than what had been expected by the Chengdu Municipal People's Government and the central government. On the same day, a summing-up meeting was convened by the Chengdu Municipal People's Government. Generally speaking, it was a great success. However, this "fire" for construction land target dealings was extinguished when a survey group of seven inspectors from the Regulation and Monitoring Department of the Ministry of Land and Resources (including Zhang Wanli) arrived in Chengdu and inquired the officials with the Chengdu Municipal Bureau of Land and Resources about the situation of rural land consolidation and local land quota dealings on Dec. 24, 2010.

Table 6.2 Statistics of the first auction of land targets for construction at the Chengdu agriculture equity exchange

Buyer	Area (μ)	Price (CNY/μ)	Total price (CNY)
Poly real Estate group Co., Ltd.	100	700,000	271,000,000
	100	690,000	
	200	660,000	
Risesun real estate development Co., Ltd.	10	780,000	135,700,000
	20	820,000	
	50	850,000	
	100	690,000	
Gemdale group	200	680,000	136,000,000
China National Petroleum Corporation (CNPC)	20	840,000	16,800,000
Others	1200		898,300,000
Total	2000		1,457,800,000

In an interview, an official with the Chengdu Agriculture Equity Exchange said: "it is just like going on a roller coaster. Just in a minute, it fell from the sky to the floor".

6.3.1 Utilization Ratification Supersedes Admittance Ratification for Land Quota Trade in Chengdu

In a circular issued by the Chengdu Municipal Bureau of Land and Resources [CHENG NONG JIAO ZHI BIAO GAO No. 005 (2010)] as of 15 Dec., 2010, it is announced that the second target auction should be held on Dec. 29, 2010, and 3000 μ of land for construction would be listed. However, in view of the booming dealings concluded in the previous auction held on Dec. 17, a survey group under the Ministry of Land and Resources made a field survey in Chengdu. It was followed by a circular issued by Chengdu Agriculture Equity Exchange as of 28 Dec., announcing that the second auction should be postponed, and there would be a further notice on the specific time of resumption. It received extensive solicitude from the media. According to not a few reports, it was stated by the Ministry of Land and Resources that the suspension of land quota dealings was fundamentally caused by its violation of the increase and decrease-linking policy.

On 14 Apr., 2011, five months after the issuance of the circular on revising the provisions on admittance ratification on Nov. 16, 2010, the Chengdu Agriculture Equity Exchange issued a third circular on the rules of land quota dealings, i.e., the *Circular on Implementing the Utilization Ratification System for the Use Right of state-owned Land for Profit-Oriented Construction*. It proclaims that the utilization ratification system for use rights of state-owned land for profit-oriented construction shall be implemented as of April 15, 2011. Different from the previous principle of admittance ratification, the utilization ratification system provides that "according to provisions under the *Implementing Opinions on Improving the Construction Land Target Exchange System and Promoting Comprehensive Rural Land Consolidation* (viz. the No. 80 document issued by the Bureau of Land and Resources Chengdu in 2011), the utilization ratification system for use rights of state-owned land for profit-oriented construction shall be implemented with the approval of the Chengdu Municipal People's Government, with the view of further enhancing the basic role of the market in resources allocation and building a land market conductive to the coordinated development of urban and rural areas". Specifically, the "bidder" thereunder is superseded by "bid winner", and different requirements are proposed for different regions. "In the first auction of use rights of state-owned land for construction (industrial land exclusive) in Jinjiang District, Qingyang District, Jinniu District, Wuhou District, Chenghua District, New Hi-Tech District, Qingbaijiang District, Longquanyi District, Wenjiang District, Xindu District, Pi County, and Shuangliu County in Chengdu City as of April 15, 2011, the *Contract for Transfer of Use rights of state-owned Land for Construction* shall be signed by the bid winners on the strength of necessary targets for the corresponding area of construction land; and in the first auction of use rights of state-owned land for construction (industrial land exclusive) in Pengzhou City, Dujiangyan City, Chongzhou City, Qionglai City, Dayi County, Jintang County, Xinjin County, and Pujiang County, the bid winner shall effect payments for the targets for the corresponding area of construction land as per the current minimum conservation price standard for construction land targets, as determined by the Chengdu Municipal People's Government prior to the signature of the *Contract for Transfer of Use rights of state-owned Land for Construction*". Moreover, the bars on land targets not to be listed for the first time are also lifted by invalidating the provision that "in the transfer of use rights of state-owned land for profit-oriented construction (not to be listed for the first time) through consolidation in Chengdu, the bid winner shall not be required to procure the corresponding land targets for construction or effect payments for such targets". Regarding how to procure the necessary targets, it is stipulated that without major modification, "the land targets for construction may be procured through either comprehensive rural land consolidation or concluding dealings and effecting due payments at the Chengdu Land & Mineral Rights Trading Center or the Chengdu Agriculture Equity Exchange".

As admittance ratification had been superseded by utilization ratification, only the "bid winner" was required to procure a target certificate, rather than all the "bidders" involved in the auction of state-owned land for profit-oriented construction. This indicates that anyone could participate in the bidding even without procuring land targets for construction, until he/she wins a bid.

6.3.2 Target Price and New Inter-regional Mechanism Under the Increase and Decrease-Linking Policy

According to the *Implementing Opinions on Improving the Construction Land Target Transaction System and Promoting Comprehensive Rural Land Consolidation* promulgated by the Chengdu Municipal Bureau of Land and Resources (viz. The No. 80 docuemnt issued by the Bureau of Land and Resources Chengdu in 2011) as of 13 Apr., 2011, "land targets for construction shall be priced through mutual negotiations between both parties according to market rules, based on the minimum conservation rate, e determined and publicized by the Chengdu Municipal People's Government yearly on Jan. 1, with considerations given to the costs of the comprehensive rural land consolidation project, including rural infrastructure, public service facilities, saturation of demands on air/water tightness and performance in wind pressure resistance and plane deformation for rural housing, etc. The minimum conservation price of land targets for construction in 2011 was CNY 180,000/μ". Meanwhile, the land targets shall be subject to a designated effective term, for it was provided by the Chengdu Municipal Bureau of Land and Resources that "the land target for construction shall remain in force for 2 years as of the date of exchange and registration and, if it remains unused during the said effective period, shall be repurchased by an agency designated by the Chengdu Municipal People's Government as per the minimum conservation price of the year".

Under the provisions on target transaction newly promulgated as of April 14, 2011, different approaches to target procurement were designated for land blocks with different attributes in different regions. Specifically, for construction land within the second ring, including 5 districts/municipalities/counties in or near the main urban zone, an auction should be held based on the principle of the highest bidder; for land blocks outside the second ring but within the third ring, the targets could be procured by direct payment at a fixed rate (in 2011, the updated price was CNY 180,000/μ); and land newly added through reconstruction of the old city town as originally owned by the State for construction could be spared from the necessity of procuring targets for construction. Thus, a new linking and classification mechanism with respect to target purchase and utilization had been established based on the price of land targets for construction. Intuitively, targets for land blocks within the second ring shall be awarded to the respective highest bidders, which would lead to a further increase in land costs; for land blocks outside the second ring but within the third ring, the targets may be procured by direct payment at a fixed rate; and land newly added through reconstruction of the old city town as originally owned by the State for construction could be spared from the necessity of procuring targets for construction (Fig. 6.3).

6.3.3 Future Development Trend

According to the *Implementing Opinions on Improving the Construction Land Target Exchange System and Promoting Comprehensive Rural Land Consolidation* (viz. the No. 80 document issued by the Bureau of Land and Resources Chengdu in 2011) promulgated by the Chengdu Municipal Bureau of Land and Resources as of April 13, 2011, land targets for construction shall be obtained through comprehensive rural land consolidation and correspond to the area of reclaimed rural construction land that has been disused minus the resettlement residential area, reserved land for the development of rural collectives and the remaining construction land as accepted. The supply of construction land targets can only be maintained on the premise of increasing efforts on reclamation under no matter admittance ratification or utilization ratification. This indicates that more and more farmers will lose their homestead and resettle in a concentrated community. In 2009, the Chengdu Municipal Bureau of Land and Resources promulgated the *White Book for Comprehensive Rural Land Consolidation in Chengdu* (2009–2015) with the view of consolidating altogether more than 5 million μ of agricultural land and over 0.5 million construction land. It is expected to increase land targets for construction by 368,000 μ and enhance the living conditions of 615,000 farmer households. To this end, the common approach is to provide a concentrated community for resettlement, mostly multi-storied buildings. Note that this is not what we mean by urban expansion or land requisition in suburbs in the

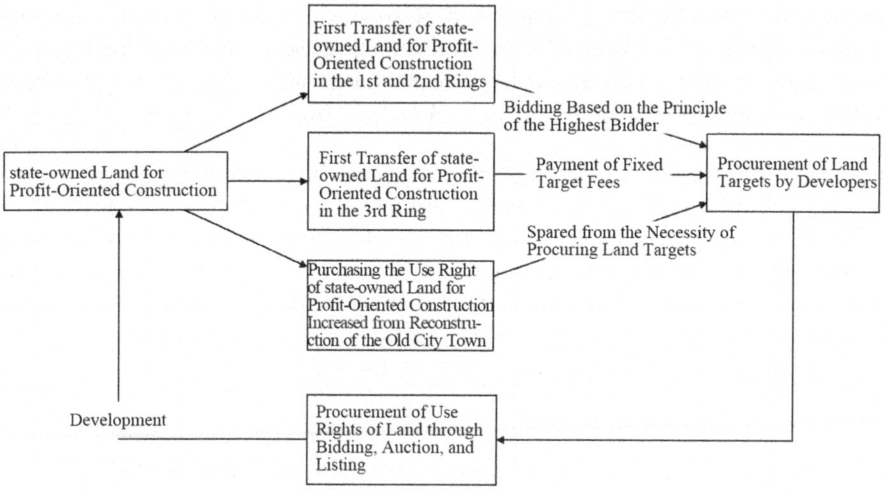

Fig. 6.3 Target exchange classification mechanism under utilization ratification in Chengdu

国有经营性建设用地：state-owned Land for Profit-Oriented Construction

开发：Development

一二圈城购买国有经营性建设用地首次出让：First Transfer of state-owned Land for Profit-Oriented Construction in the 1st and 2nd Rings

三圈城购买国有经营性建设用地首次出让：First Transfer of state-owned Land for Profit-Oriented Construction in the 3rd Ring

购买旧城改造出的国有建设用地使用权：Purchasing the Use Right of state-owned Land for Profit-Oriented Construction Increased from Reconstruction of the Old City Town

竞价购买指标价高者得：Bidding Based on the Principle of the Highest Bidder

缴纳固定指标费：Payment of Fixed Target Fees

不需要获得用地指标：Spared from the Necessity of Procuring Land Targets

开发主体获得建设用地指标：Procurement of Land Targets by Developers

招、拍、挂等程序获得该地块土地使用权：Procurement of Use Rights of Land through Bidding, Auction, and Listing

conventional sense, but the tendency that more and more farmers move from rural areas to the city and change their residential patterns. In this context, the urbanization is understood from the perspective of land targets.

Now the exchange rules for construction land targets at the Chengdu Agriculture Land Exchange have been reviewed briefly. Based on our investigation, it is found that the various land consolidation projects in Chengdu can be classified into high and low-level linking projects. "High-level linking projects" shall be subject to the approval by the Ministry of Land and Resources based on the increase and decrease-linking policy; while a "low-level linking project" may be established on the strength of corresponding land quota purchased at the Chengdu Agriculture Equity Exchange and registration with the Chengdu Municipal Bureau of Land and Resources, independent of the pilot projects under the Ministry of Land and Resources. This means that the target exchange may be allowed to proceed without the necessity of providing a resettlement residential area for farmers in advance or being submitted to the competent department of land and resources for verification, as stipulated by the Ministry of Land and Resources. Therefore, based on this classification method and how it has been implemented in various regions, the inter-project boundary has been gradually blurred by local governments, leading to an increasingly intensified local autonomy on the whole.

6.4 Project Logic of Local Governments: A Case Study of the Situation in Dayi County, Chengdu

The system of linking the increase in land used for urban construction and the decrease in land used for rural construction has run within the project scheme. With the foothold secured at the village level, this system is basically implemented by the people's government at the county/township level. The logic in the practices of local governments may be inferred from an analysis of the considerations during the specific project operations under the people's government at the county/township level, according to our survey of the situation in Dayi County, Chengdu City. In short, during the specific operations, what local governments care the most is how to complete the project as perfectly as possible with limited financial resources. From the perspective of macro-structure, the increase and decrease-linking policy and other land-related policies as discussed earlier, as well as the new changes in the relationship between the central government and local governments as highlighted in our analysis, all emerged under the background of the project scheme. Similar to the well-known unit system and the double-track system, it is a system where the entire social structure and mechanism are integrated. In this sense, it refers to neither the operation process of a single project, nor the various project management systems, but a governance model in which the relationship among people's governments at various levels and the various sectors in the society can be integrated. The project scheme is not only a system, an operations-enabling mechanism, but also a project-centered thinking model by which the strategies and tactics of the State, social groups and individuals on how to make decisions and act are made. Under the background of governance under the project scheme, "project economy" has become an incentive mechanism to mobilize local governments. Meanwhile, it also urges the central government and local governments to go all down to the people. From the perspective of the project scheme, an analysis of the logic in of high and low-level linking practices of local governments would help us to get rid of the simple logic in the dual structure of the central government and local governments where pertinent policies are developed by the higher authorities while the localities have their counter-measures.

6.4.1 Rapid Financing: Preliminary Logic in Regions of Target Selling

For example, located in the outskirts of Chengdu City, Dayi County is relatively underdeveloped and thus faced with serious financial problems in the process of development. In particular, as a result of the Wenchuan earthquake in 2008, the post-earthquake reconstruction brought about even greater financial pressure, which, under the existing system, was transformed into huge political pressure. Considering that post-earthquake reconstruction had become an unalterable target, the local government resorted to the increase and decrease-linking policy in order to establish a contingency funding platform. In 2009, Bureau of Land and Resources of Dayi County sold out 1900 μ of land as targets under the increase and decrease-linking policy to Wenjiang and Longquanyi at Chengdu Agriculture Equity Exchange for altogether CNY 285,000,000 at CNY 150,000/μ. However, as post-earthquake reconstruction was gradually completed, the need of land targets for construction arising from challenges from local development zoomed in. Besides, as the costs of land consolidation rose steadily, the price of circulating targets under the increase and decrease-linking policy witnessed an ever-increase. Therefore, local governments became more and more aware of the role of land in the entire development process, and thus turned down the option of selling land targets to other areas in the hope of promoting their own development. In such a context, the target-selling local governments became unanimously repentant. As described by an official from Xinchang Town, Dayi County, "What can you do even with so much money? Without land targets, money cannot buy development". "Local development has been confined as a result of target drift".

6.4.2 "Pass or Fail Mark" for Admittance: Strict Budget at the Grass-Roots Level

A contract for project funds payable from fiscal revenues at the county level is usually awarded to the government at the township level responsible for organizing the implementation of the project. This process should rely on meticulous costs accounting so as to complete the project on the premise of maintaining affordability or even surplus. In accordance with the available policies in Dayi County, the per capita living space in the concentrated community was 30 m^2 and, taking infrastructure into account, the per capita land occupation was 50 m^2. On the other hand, the annual appropriation standard for land consolidation and resettlement was CNY 150,000/μ from 2008 to 2010, as enhanced to CNY 200,000/μ in 2011 and further to

CNY 250,000/μ in 2012. According to the reference standard the average per capita surplus circulating targets for construction shall be 103 m^2 (0.15 μ). However, as a result of the varied terrain and development status, there was a huge difference in the costs of dismantlement and construction among the villages and towns. In order to strictly control the costs within the appropriations from fiscal revenues at the county level, for example, CNY 250,000/μ as appropriated in 2012, a "pass or fail mark" has usually been drawn to determine whether a farmer household could be included in the project under the increase and decrease-linking policy, according to the situation of the township where they live. This "pass or fail mark" should correspond to a designated volume of surplus land targets for construction obtained from relocation of farmer households. This means that an average per capita surplus of land targets of 103 m^2 should be maintained, given the average standard stipulated by the people's government at the county level as the "pass or fail mark". Otherwise, the shortage should be covered with due payments. On the other hand, in case of any surplus beyond the stipulated standard, the compensation would also be enhanced accordingly. This is what local officials actually meant by "the principle of over-compensation for any over-surplus or a supplemental payment for any deficiency". However, in some areas confined by the relatively high average costs of a land consolidation project, say, the mountainous Xilin Town, the calculated standard for average per capita surplus of land targets for construction was enhanced to 135 m^2, leading to an extremely limited amount of farmer households who could be included in the project under the increase and decrease-linking policy, because the per capita occupied land has reached 185 m^2 in some cases (50 m^2 for resettlement plus 135 m^2 as per the stipulated standard). Thus, we can understand the strict budget of township governments. The key to drawing a "pass or fail mark" is cost accounting. In this process, the people's government at the township level would usually do as it sees fit with the quantitative appropriation per μ from fiscal revenues at the provincial, municipal, county levels.

6.4.3 Bundling Project Scheme: A Time and Effort-Saving Approach

Appropriations from fiscal revenues at the county level have usually been subject to a lump sum contract that is far from enough. For example, the lump sum appropriation for Dayi County was CNY 250,000/μ in 2012, and the stipulated standard for surplus of land targets for construction was 103 m^2 per capita. However, according to our survey in Xinchang Town, the costs calculated by the local residents reached CNY 307,000/μ, as shown in Table 6.3. Moreover, unforeseeable expenses were not calculated, including costs of designed track reconstruction, bridges and tomb relocation within the concentrated community for resettlement, as the case may be. The majority of other townships in Dayi County were basically the same case. In short, CNY 250,000 would be far from enough or "profitable". So, how can we make up for it?

Table 6.3 Cost accounting for comprehensive land consolidation in Xinchang town under the increase and decrease-linking policy

Item	Standard	Cost per Capita	Cost per μ
Land ownership/use rights adjustment costs	CNY 46,000/μ	CNY 3450 per capita	CNY 46,000/μ * 50 m^2/666.67 m^2/0.15 μ = CNY 23,000/μ
Compensation for relocation	CNY 10,000 per capita	CNY 10,000 per capita	CNY 10,000/0.15 μ = CNY 67,000/μ
Landscape engineering costs	CNY 4,000 per capita (0.15 μ)	CNY 4000 per capita	CNY 4000/0.15 μ = CNY 26,700/μ
Costs of leveling and infrastructure	CNY 12,000 per capita (0.15 μ)	CNY 12,000 per capita	CNY 12,000/0.15 μ = CNY 80,000/μ
Compensation for ground attachments	CNY 200,000/m^2	CNY 3060 per capita	(CNY 200,000/m^2 * 153 m^2)/0.15 μ = CNY 20,400/μ
Reclamation costs	CNY 7000/μ	CNY 1610 per capita	(CNY 7,000/μ * 153 m^2/666.67 m^2)/0.15 μ = CNY 10,700/μ
Miscellaneous	Expenses incurred in topographic survey, evaluation, exploration, planning, design, construction, acceptance, etc.	CNY 2754 per capita	CNY 12,000/μ
Financing costs	18%	CNY 9700 per capita	CNY 42,200/μ
Working fund		CNY 5740 per capita	CNY 25,000/μ
Total		CNY 52,314 per capita	CNY 307,000/μ

According to our survey, local governments usually resort to the bundling project scheme in order to ensure the completion of the project while keeping it out of the red or even profitable. (a) Bundle up multiple land blocks where old buildings shall be dismantled as a single project under the increase and decrease-linking policy. To some extent, the costs of packaging arising from planning, design, exploration, acceptance, etc. may be reduced, and public infrastructure may be shared by all the near-by communities. (b) Bundle up multiple concentrated communities under various "names". Just like "twisting thousands of lines into a single rope", this approach, is in concert with policy and financial support and highly cost-effective. As our survey in Wangsi Town indicates, Wangcheng Block in Yixing Village accommodated 90 farmer households relocated to make room for a metallurgical demonstration plant and also some others included in the "concentrated resettlement in multi-storied buildings" in the pure sense. And the construction project for a concentrated block in Futian Village also bundled up Project No. 2923, the Chengpu Railway Construction Project, the New Countryside Building Project, among others, (c) Bundle up the projects under the increase and decrease-linking policy and other industrial development and construction projects. To this end, social capital would be involved in the development of surplus land for construction to alleviate the financial pressure. For example, in the Jiudong Bridge Joint-Construction Project in Xinchang Town, it was provided that "70% of the land newly increased relocation of farmer households should be used for resettlement, and the remainder used by the investors to develop a rural tourism project". The "price difference" arising from the construction of the resettlement block and even some other "burdens" would be borne by the developer.

6.4.4 Maximizing Circulating Quotas: An Inevitable Choice by Local Governments

In the framework of the increase and decrease-linking policy, extra-budgetary land targets have provided an effective incentive mechanism to local governments. In the sense of a standardized project under the increase and decrease-linking policy, local governments would be more than often motivated to involve themselves in relevant projects in order to procure land targets necessary for urban construction. According to the design of the land target exchange platforms in Chengdu and Chongqing, inter-regional targets "drift"-driven trade is permitted. Therefore, in the practices of no matter selling targets for immediate financing or involving the "pass or fail mark" and/or the "bundling project scheme" in order to complete the project in a cost-effective manner, the ultimate purpose is to maximize the benefits from circulating targets as possible. It is safe to say that this is an inevitable choice for local governments. In this sense, the goal of the increase or decrease-linking policy at the outset, namely "increase in land", has become a by-product. Local governments involved in the implementation of the increase or decrease-linking policy, especially those in areas where old buildings shall be dismantled, would suffer from high costs, compared with the expected proceeds. Therefore, the newly increased

Table 6.4 Elementary statistics of comprehensive land consolidation projects under the increase and decrease-linking policy in Anren town in 2010. (6 April, 2010)

Basic situation of land blocks where old buildings shall be dismantled				Number of projects	Basic situation of resettlement blocks for farmers						Circulating land targets for construction under the policy (*unit μ*)	Newly increased effective cultivated land (*unit μ*)
Village (community)	Area	Number of relocated households	Number of relocated farmers		S. N.	Resettlement block	Location	Area (*unit μ*)	Accomodation capacity (*unit* household)	Accomodation capacity (*unit* people)		
Changfu, Xinhe, Wuxing, Sanhe, Shuanghe	880.9	786	2677	1	1	Sanhe	Sanhe community	30.3	109	369	656.8	1.5
					2	Xintuan (a)	Xintuan village	195.7	594	2007		
					3	Xinhe	Xinhe village	29.3	86	301		
Chenhe, Jintang, Shiwa	985.7	835	2921	1	1	Chenhe	Jintang community, Chenhe village	214.2	628	2197	720.7	2.3
					2	Shiwa	Shiwa village	70.6	207	724		
Yumin, Xintuan, Qinian, Jinguang	403.3	399	1452	1	1	Xintuan (b)	Xintuan village	141.6	399	1452	278.5	1.2

land would never be retained as cultivated land. According to a survey in Anren Town, Dayi County, in 2010, the surplus land targets newly increased from three major comprehensive land consolidation projects under the increase and decrease-linking policy reached 656.8, 720.7 and 278.5 μ, with merely 1.5, 2.3 and 1.2 μ of effective cultivated land retained, respectively. It should be emphasized that our discussion is aimed at a review of the logical relationship, rather than discriminating a "good government" from the "bad" (Table 6.4).

6.5 Rapid Expansion of Local Financing Platforms & Large-Scale Capital Investment in Rural Areas

In the existing development model, local governments shall foremost address the demands on land and capital. In the "trinity" of land, fiscal revenues and finance, land is undoubtedly the foundation. For no matter local governments or capital, the fundamental concern is not land itself, but the associated assets and its capital value. The rise of local financing platforms is an inevitable outcome of this development logic and model.

In particular, the central government launched the CNY 4 trillion economic stimulus plan in November 2008, including CNY 280 billion for affordable housing projects, CNY 370 billion for rural livelihood projects and rural infrastructure construction, CNY 1. 8 trillion for the construction of railway, highway, airport, urban and rural power grid, CNY 40 billion for health, culture and education undertakings, CNY 350 billion for environmental investment, CNY 160 billion for independent innovation and structural adjustment, and CNY 1 trillion for post-disaster recovery and reconstruction. It can be seen that this is essentially an investment driven program. In this program, the central government came up with only CNY 1. 8 trillion, so local governments had to resort to financing channels in order to raise the remaining CNY 3.2 trillion. Thus, the year 2009 witnessed a vigorous campaign of financing, resulting in an explosive growth in the debts of local governments. At the beginning of 2008, the total liabilities of financing platforms run by local governments were only approximately CNY 1 trillion; however, stimulated by the CNY 4 trillion economic stimulus plan, coupled with the easing monetary and lending policies, "the total number of government-run financing platforms in China has increased sharply to more than 3000 (it is also heard to be more than 8000), of which more than 70% are run at the county/district level, and the debt balance has also increased from slightly over CNY 1000 billion to more than CNY 6000 billion (it is also said to be more than CNY 5000 billion, and according to relevant sources, it is even estimated at CNY 11,000 billion), of which the majority are due to banks". Well-known is the extensive involvement of local governments. Running these financing platforms, local governments are actually the debtors. As of the end of 2012, in the 84 major cities of China, altogether 348,700 hectares of land was under mortgage for a loan of CNY 5.

95 trillion in total, with a year-on-year increase rate of 15.7 and 23.2%, respectively. On the one hand, local debts have been expanded ever since; on the other hand, the repayment of debt balance from revenues from land transfer witnessed significant increase in some regions. According to an audit report on the debts of 36 local governments since 2011 released by the National Audit Office of People's Republic of China in June 2013, as of the end of 2012, 4 provincial units and 17 provincial capitals have promised to repay CNY 774,697 billion of the debt balance from fiscal revenues from land transfer, accounting for 54.64% of the total debt balance of these regions.

However, according to Liu Shouying, et al., the existing land selling mode is hardly sustainable. As a result of the rise in the expenses arising from land requisition and relocation in recent years, the disposable land revenues (i.e., the so-called "land fiscal revenues") of local governments shrank rapidly, accompanied by an ever-decrease in the year-on-year growth rate. In 2008, the actually disposable revenues of local governments from land transfer totaled CNY 436.4 billion, accounting for 43.9% of the total revenues from land transfer; in 2012, these two figures were CNY 626.8 billion (with a year-on-year decrease of CNY 317.2 billion) and 21.7%, respectively. Institutional arrangements that rely on "land fiscal revenues" to cover security for the people's livelihood and other expenses would necessarily entail unsustainability. First and foremost, the volatile revenues from land transfer are unreliable in view of the fixed expenses arising from or in relation to the people's livelihood. In case of any substantial drop in land revenues, it would be difficult for local governments to honor their commitment to the livelihood of the people. Besides, the sharp rise in the costs of land requisition would lead to a continual decline in the proportion of revenues from land transfer to the total revenues, which will have a direct impact on the supportability for people's livelihood.

Sustainable land-centered development shall rely on not only continuous increase of land targets but also a steady inflow of capital. For example, according to the Overall Planning Committee of Dayi County, as a result of the large population, weak economic foundation, and high demands on investment in agriculture, countryside and farmers, livelihood projects, etc., Dayi County had been underfinanced and suffered from prominent contradictions between fiscal revenues and expenditures; on the other hand, the austerity measures adopted by the State whereby mortgage financing was relatively limited (especially for those projects in need of large-scale gage) and the limited available state-owned land that may be used under mortgage had led to huge difficulties in financing. Some financing platforms, underfunded as they were, could not satisfy the requirements for bank lending. Thus, the difficulties were even aggravated. Besides, the inadequate project funding, especially for traffic construction, land consolidation, township reconstruction, forestry management, concentrated communities for resettlement and infrastructure, etc., called for large-scale external input of capital. So how can we raise such money? Actually, it had been partially made up by the appropriations under the project scheme and, more importantly, by financing through local financial mortgage platforms and involving massive social capital in different projects by means of applying the increase and decrease-linking policy and establishing a market resources sharing mechanism between urban and rural areas, so as to ensure rational distribution of value-added benefits and effectively mobilize the market and farmers. According to the statistics of the Overall Planning Committee of Dayi County, CNY 3.1 billion of social capital was leveraged through market resources allocation for the sake of post-earthquake rehabilitation. Thus, a comprehensive campaign was launched in Taoyuan, involving 11 municipal road reconstruction, expansion and building projects in the inner city areas; a total of 26.3 km of underground pipelines were either newly built or reconstructed; the construction in 3 major towns, namely Anren, Wangsi, and Shaqu, was accelerated; 16 townships were included in the reconstruction; and 62 comprehensive land consolidation projects were completed. In 2011, 13,500 parcels were included in the rural property right transfer at a sum price of CNY 41.2 million, and 679 parcels were used as gage for a loan of CNY 110 million. As the rapid expansion of local financing platforms involved massive social capital, due attention shall be paid to how to estimate the collateral risks.

The large-scale comprehensive consolidation of rural land has been highly demanding on fund operation. As consolidation projects expanded, it became more and more difficult for local governments to satisfy the huge demands on funds. The introduction of social capital has become an inevitable choice. However, as capital is usually on the rational side, how to attract social investment has become another important issue to be addressed. In some regions, allocating partial revenues from the transfer of land targets for construction as proceeds of the social capital provided a solution. It means that the social capital not only contributed to land consolidation in rural areas, but also shared the proceeds from the transfer of land targets for urban construction. Meanwhile, along with the gradual development of funding platforms, how to provide development space for social capital in rural areas has become another issue that calls for the exploration by local governments. However, the ever-increasing involvement of social capital in the comprehensive rural land consolidation shall not be simply perceived as a solution to address financial difficulties, as the impacts of capital on our reform have been increasingly highlighted. In particular, to which degree it has affected local planning is worthy of our further study.

In a review by the new government ever since the 18th National Congress of the Communist Party of China, it is stressed that "in streamlining administration and instituting decentralization, the central government shall enforce privatization of the banking and investment mechanism; otherwise, the vacancy of competition and devolution will highlight the powers of local governments or produce even worse consequences". At this point, more emphasis is seemingly put on the role of the market mechanism for social capital. What role is played by the extensive involvement of social capital in local construction remains an open question. Will it move toward a more extensive market competition or toward a new power corpus in closer relation with local governments as a result of its continuous expansion? In light the overall operation of land projects, the latter seems to be the answer.

Therefore, the risks in relation to the involvement of social capital shall be attached with great importance.

6.6 A Discussion on the Relationship Between the Central Government and Local Governments from the Perspective of Land Policies

To a large extent, the centrally controlled resources determine the authority of the central government over local governments. Ever since the adoption of the tax-sharing system, the central government has, on the one hand, wielded huge financial control, resulting in the unprecedented centralization; on the other hand, it had to arouse the vitality of local developments. In such a context, the incentives relied on the visualization of a certain space for future development, and variations in the size of this space might reflect the evolution of the relationship between the central government and local governments. A new relationship framework has been established against the land issues under the historical background.

6.6.1 Logic of Strict Central Control

As we know, the central government is responsible for the comprehensive administration. Rural land-related issues basically have respect to social stability, cultivated land red-line, national food security, incentives for regional economic development, etc. Thus, land administration-related policies have been obviously characterized by centralization, as represented by the policy of balancing the occupation and compensation of cultivated land. The local land utilization planning and approval of state-owned land for construction have under strict control, resulting in a serious shortage of land targets necessary for local development.

6.6.2 Logic of Local Development

Compared with the central government, local developments are dedicated to less complicated objectives. Generally speaking, they have to address the economic development goals against the so-called regional championship or official promotion tournament (commonly known as the "GDP doctrine"). Since the adoption of the tax-sharing system, their pursuit of industrialization has been gradually replaced by that of urbanization. Thus, the development model centered on the trinity of land, fiscal revenues and finance has become prevalent throughout the country, with land and capital considered as the core preconditions for development.

6.6.3 Logic of Top-Down Incentives

Under the centralized system, how to maintain the motivation of local developments is a frequent topic for discussion. Regarding land issues, on the one hand, strict control has been imposed by the central government; on the other hand, a certain space or motivation for reform should be provided to local governments. The policy of linking the increase in land used for urban construction and the decrease in land used for rural construction truly eased the tension in the regulation of land issues, allowing local governments to carry out reforms under the premise of keeping the red line of cultivated land.

6.6.4 Logic of Local Governments in Solidifying Benefits from the Reform

As a "leeway" has been opened for land-related issues under central policies, the local development-oriented reform has been justified to some extent. However, we have felt a impulse to go beyond the framework of reform in a pursuit of even more preferential policies to support local development (dominated by urbanization). On the one hand, operations beyond the existing reform pilot framework have been prevalent in various regions; on the other hand, local governments are actively negotiating with the people's governments at the next higher levels in a hope of solidifying or even expanding their share of benefits from the reform.

To be frank, the increase and decrease-linking policy is an inevitable choice for the central government under the background of rapid industrialization and urbanization and, of course, there was no alternative to maintain the initiatives of local governments and broaden the horizon for development. During the game between the central government and local governments, although principally reserved by the central government, the political powers over "ultimate sanction" and personnel (as emphasized by many scholars) cannot be exercised easily or frequently, not to mention running through the specific administrative process. Thus, within the framework of centralization, local governments have gradually become dominant, even though the central government still holds the position of authority over taxation and personnel. Therefore, it has become of great significance (while increasingly difficult) to control the size and tightness of the "tap" opened by the central government under relevant policies for the local pilot reform.

The manner of playing this game between the central government and local governments and the results depend on the respective authority of the people's governments at all levels.

Chapter 7
Relationship Between the Central Government and Local Governments & Urbanization

We have examined the evolution of the relationship between the central government and local governments based on a scrutiny of the fiscal system and land administration of China in the previous chapters. On the whole, local governments have become more and more dependent on land development and land fiscal revenues in their pursuit of local development ever since the implementation of the tax-sharing system. The central government regulate the speed of local development and adjust inter-regional balance by imposing control over land quotas. Thus, the central government and local governments have gradually gained their relatively independent subject consciousness. Their relationship in the new era can be understood based on development objectives and local benefits.

Since the radical economic stimulus plan was introduced by the central government in 2008, dramatic changes have occurred to both the fiscal system and land administration. Local governments attempted to go beyond the control of the central government over land by manipulating the increase and decrease-related policy. Furthermore, local governments established numerous local financing platforms to accomodate the large-scale bank financing by land mortgage in order to promote urban construction. In such a context, the urbanization has been basically motivated by the "trinity" of land, fiscal revenues and finance.

7.1 Urbanization Driven by the "Trinity" of Land, Fiscal Revenues and Bank Investments

How did the local governments raise the funds necessary for urban construction? According to our survey, the funds for constructing urban infrastructure in Shaoxing County and Jinhua City, Zhejiang Province came from government investment (fiscal appropriations +land use right transfer fees) and financing. The former accounted for approximately 1/3 of the funds, while the latter 2/3. It is obvious that

F. Zhou and M. Tan, *Relationship between the Central Government and Local Governments of Contemporary China*, Social Development Experiences in China,
DOI 10.1007/978-981-10-4388-8_7

the real pillar supporting urban development and construction was financing, rather than financial fund.

Generally speaking, government-run financing platforms may procure bank loans via three approaches: mutual guarantee, financial security and land mortgage. In the case of mutual guarantee, several large-scale government-run enterprises provide guarantee for each other with capital in cash that is mostly sourced from fiscal appropriations by the government, so any loan obtained in such a way is essentially under the guarantee of fiscal appropriations. Financial security simply requires the competent bureau of finance under the people's government to directly provide guarantee in the form of a letter of commitment specifying the subject of loans, subject of guarantee and various other details. Under the guarantee of fiscal appropriations, these two approaches are basically the same. It is worth mentioning that the Security—Law of the PRC prohibits the government to be the subject of guarantee for loans. Thus land mortgage via financing platforms has become the government's most frequently-adopted approach to procure funds.

Loans secured by land mortgage shall be granted only under the premise of submitting a certificate for land use right. In the regions investigated in this study, local governments usually allot land use right for either non-profit or profit-oriented commercial/residential construction to the developers, despite of minor difference in the procedures. Regarding land to be used for profit-oriented commercial/residential construction, government-run enterprises shall use it as mortgage to obtain bank loans, rather than transfer it under the bidding, auction and listing system.

During land development and urban construction, "land-for-land" has been widely practised, where public welfare lands at convenient locations are transferred for profit-oriented construction based on the bidding, auction and listing system in order to cover the expenditures of utilities with the land use right transfer fees. This idea has been copied by government-run enterprises in their practices of using land as mortgage for bank loans, except that the land blocks at convenient locations are not used for profit-oriented construction, but as bank mortgage at a high rate, which is actually the financial version of "land-for-land".

The financial version of "land-for-land" is suitable for not only government-run enterprises, but also government departments aiming at land development, urban construction and industrial management. The significance of land finance lies in that local governments rely on land mortgage-based financing in not only urban development and infrastructure construction, but also land requisition, development of new zones as well as the construction of industrial parks.

In addition to government-invested enterprises, the land reserve center also plays an important role in the profit-oriented operations of local governments. The land reserve system is designed to make good use of land reserves of state-owned enterprises to be restructured so as to address the livelihood demands of laid-off workers, under which the land reserves shall be mainly sourced from the back-purchase of state-owned land reserves. However, it is found in our survey that in practice, the land reserved by governments has been extended so far beyond the design that the requisition of land owned by farmer collectives became a highlight. Their motive for these moves can be further demonstrated by the uses of land reserves. The non-profitable public construction and industrial land is excluded from the supply list of the land reserve center. Almost all of the land reserves are used for residential and commercial purposes in order to maximize the revenues from land.

Based on the analysis of land mortgage above, another kind of relationship between land finance and local fiscal revenues can be perceived: as more and more banks loans secured by land have been granted to the land reserve center which, in turn, has been engaged in ongoing capitalization from land development and transfer. The concept of working of the center was to invest loans secured by mortgage of land reserves on land requisition, thereby allowing repayment from revenues therefrom and the use of requisitioned land as mortgage in another round of loan application.

In such a way, the financial capital, as "lubricants" facilitating land acquisition, development and transfer, enables the government to quickly expand land development and accumulate huge revenues. These land revenues, as indicated in the foregoing analysis, have been mostly invested in urbanization. In this cycle, both the government and the bank are fully aware that loans secured by land mortgage would be usually repaid within 1–2 years, and those secured by fiscal appropriations are subject to a longer repayment term but still reliable on account of governmental guarantee with fiscal revenues. The fiscal revenues of Chinese government are mainly constituted by revenues from land transfer and taxes. Huge revenues may be obtained from land transfer as long as land requisition and transfer are sustainable or charge a high price. As indicated in the previous analysis, as more and more fiscal revenues and financial capital are invested in urban construction and infrastructure expansion, the taxes paid to local governments, especially those levied on construction, real estate and other pillar industries would ever increase, accompanied by enhanced financial solvency of the local governments, though these will come at the cost of an enlarged financing scale. Further, the growth of government revenues will expand not only financing, but also land requisition. Thus, this is actually a "win-win" formula. Therefore, it can be seen that land revenues, bank loans, urban construction and land requisition have formed an ever-rolling and ever-enlarging circle that produces not only enormous financial resources for local governments, but also the prosperity of industrialization and urbanization typical of the 21st Century. The urbanization process driven by the "trinity" of land, fiscal revenues and finance is illustrated below (Fig. 7.1).

As the major driving force for urbanization ever since the beginning of the 21st Century interwoven with the city and land operating behaviors of local government, this trinity has promoted not only the rapid and continuous growth of GDP and fiscal revenues, but also the prosperity of urbanization.

"Land urbanization" mainly includes three stages. On the first stage, agricultural land is requisitioned for urban construction and thus generates substantial revenues

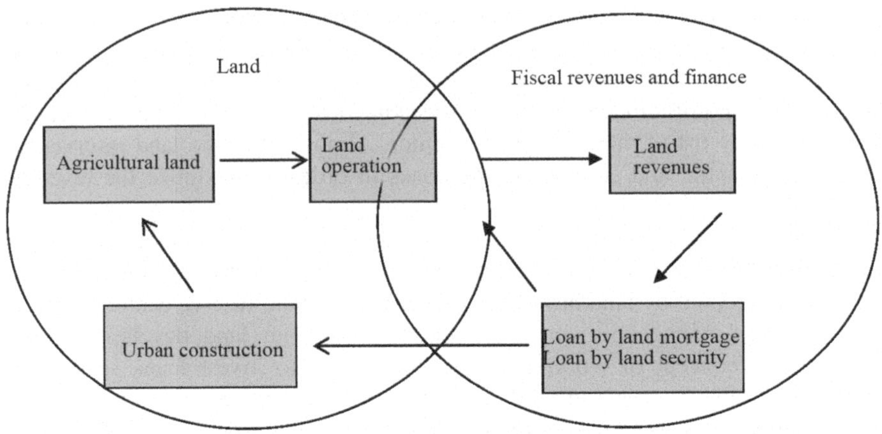

Fig. 7.1 Urbanization driven by the "trinity" of land, fiscal revenues and bank investments

for local governments. On the second stage, land revenues are used as the capital to establish local government-run financing platforms, thereby leveraging enormous financial capital for land development and urban construction. On the third stage, the expansion of urban construction greatly stimulates the demands on state-owned land for construction, making it necessary to develop and requisition both unused lands and lands which are used inefficiently in urban areas and agricultural land, thereby launching a new circle that starts from land and, with fiscal revenues as the intermediate carrier, and ends at finance.

This development mode gave birth to a vigorous urbanization which is essentially centered on land (rather than industries and population) and thus referred to as "land urbanization" in this book. This mode of development has the following features:

First, industrialization is not a premise of land urbanization. Of course, this does not mean that industrialization is not important, but that urbanization is not the major concern of industrialization. The urbanization in east China is characterized by a close correlation between land urbanization and industrialization as well as a vacancy of massive inflow and prosperity of export-oriented industrial enterprises, deviating from the trinity-driven development mode. However, a review of the development process in various regions shows that the key to urbanization is the real estate industry. As long as fiscal and financial support is ready, the real estate industry can be developed independently without relying on industrialization, leading to real estate bubbles.

Urban expansion in this phase is mainly characterized by the sharp increase in land used for urban construction (most notably, for residential and commercial construction as well as utilities), rather than in industrial land. Real estate development, in place of industrialization, has become the foundation of urban development and expansion. As long as urban land is priced high enough, banks are usually interested in lending, thereby providing fiscal and financial means for local governments to comprehensively promote the development of urban economy. This economic development mode, characterized by urban expansion, is basically aimed at a growth of GDP and fiscal revenues and mainly relies on governmental investment in public facilities with revenues from land requisition, development and transfer, whereby the real estate industry gradually takes over the vital role of industrialization in promoting urbanization.

Second, population urbanization is also excluded from the necessary conditions for land urbanization. Normally, urbanization relies on industrialization to accumulate necessary capital. The labor forces necessarily involved in industrialization and their family members constitute the population basis for urban development. The production and consumption behaviors of these people are considered as the main part of urban operations. However, China has taken a different urbanization path. Most of the massive labor forces are not urbanized, but "migrant workers" in want of the permanent urban residence certificate and the status of a citizen. Their family members still live in the rural areas in the Midwest. Therefore, such semi-urbanization short of urbanizing migrant farmer-workers has not only resulted in the dualistic pattern of social groups characterized by huge differences between urban residents and migrant-workers in both incomes and social status, but also brought about hundreds of millions of migrant population separated from their families. As migrant workers, their parents and children are far away from one another, which will result in many new social problems in the long run.

There are at least three reasons for this situation. First, the dual household registration system of urban and rural areas stands as an institutional factor. Since it is not the focus of our analysis, we won't linger on it. It should be noted that while the housing prices are soaring, even if the dual household registration system is abolished, migrant workers still cannot be urbanized and thus will be inevitably homeless in the cities for which they work. Therefore, under the current situation, the household registration system is no longer a key issue for urbanization. Second, the "labor-intensive" export-oriented economic strategy, suitable for making full use of the surplus labor under China's characteristic conditions as it is, pre-defines a long-standing low laborage for migrant workers with the manufacturing industry in urban areas under the premise of "an unlimited supply of labor". These secondary citizens are even ineligible to file an application for low-rent housing. It is impossible for them to afford the rents. Moreover, the urbanization model typical of the 21st Century has become more and more dependent on the real estate industry, rather than industrialization. Driven by the trinity of land, fiscal revenues and finance, the prices of land/housing and costs of living in urban areas have been skyrocketing, thereby basically ruling out the possibility for industrial workers to settle down in the cities where they work.

Finally, land urbanization stands on the trinity of land, fiscal revenues and finance. As such, it would bring about a significant increase in fiscal revenues and energize the flow of financial loans as well as rapid urban construction. Compared with other development paths, this is the easiest and most cost-effective in terms of political performance.

7.2 "Concentrated Resettlement of Farmers in Multi-Storied Buildings" and "Capital Investment in Rural Areas"

As a result of the exploration of land-centered urbanization in East China, land urbanization has become less correlated with industrialization and population urbanization. Furthermore, we now know the combination of capital and land can directly stimulate capital accumulation and rapid urbanization. This may explain the reason of booming land urbanization in the central and western regions unaccompanied by population concentration and rapid industrialization. In the following sections, we will use the situation in Chengdu to illustrate the impacts of this urbanization on farmers.

In 2007, the Comprehensive Reform Pilot Area for National Overall Planning of Urban and Rural Areas was formally established in Chengdu in order to furtherize the reform of property right system, explore a new mechanism of rural land administration, forge a set of characteristic and comprehensive reform models distinguished by "overall planning, centralization, large-scale circulation", and carry out a comprehensive reform, mainly including land consolidation, concentrated farmers resettlement as well as the reform of the rural property right system. As such, the core idea was to increase land for urban and rural construction by means of land consolidation and concentrated farmers resettlement, and to address the consequent issues regarding social security, employment, lifestyle changes, etc.

The important impacts of overall planning for urban and rural areas can be summarized as "concentrated resettlement of farmers in multi-storied buildings" and "capital investment in the countryside". The former refers to villages merger and concentrated habitation, while the latter means lease-based scale operations by agricultural enterprises are encouraged, for, as a result of the concentrated resettlement, the original contracted land is too far to be cultivated. This process is initiated by government via fiscal and financial means.

Homestead reclamation following the concentrated resettlement of farmers in multi-storied buildings would allow an increase in cultivated land under the premise of breaching no state-designated cultivated land conservation quotas. In the Comprehensive Pilot Area for the Reform of the Land System in Chengdu, such cultivated land may be requisitioned for urban construction, and the newly increased land quotas for construction are allowed to circulate within the jurisdiction of Chengdu Municipal People's Government. More accurately, saving those retained for self-utilization, newly increased land quotas for construction may be traded or replaced within "Pan-Chengdu" and thereby known as "circulating quotas" under the increase and decrease—linking policy. For the first batch of projects under the linked increase and decrease policy implemented in 8 pilot areas, including Pi County. Shuangliu. Jinjiang, and Qingbaijiang District, dismantlement and reclamation had been completed by the later half of 2009. As such, the dismantlement works involved altogether 3230 μ of residential areas, 2663 μ of land was used as circulating targets, and newly increased cultivated land within the project area amounted up to more than 2601 μ. Our survey included 12 resettled households. In addition, it is found that other districts and counties in Chengdu are engaged in similar large-scale projects.

The overall planning for urban and rural areas has been most importantly aimed at lifting constraints for land urbanization, going far beyond trading circulating land quotas. This process was led by the government through fiscal and financial means and guided by an idea basically the same with that in land urbanization in the eastern region, except that rural homestead was included.

Along with the large-scale concentrated resettlement in rural areas, the increase of the distance between farmers and arable lands as well as the year-by-year decrease of the profits of tilling the land forced most farmers to give up farming. Under the circumstances, the local governments have organized urban capital investment in the countryside and centralized circulation and lease of rural land. As the incomes from farming have been even lower than rents, land lease has been the most common option. As a result, a rush for large-scale land lease was set off in order to promote the development of modern agriculture. It is worth noting that the capital investment in modern and tourist agriculture is unprofitable or even losing money. Why were capital owners so interested in leasing cultivated land in rural areas then? As the limits on land quotas for urban construction cannot be extended, local governments launched a campaign of concentrated resettlement for farmers in order to "replace" every inch of land newly increased from rural consolidation with land quotas for construction around the city and, without taking up allotted land quotas for urban construction, satisfy the demands of developers on investment in urban construction. As a supplement to the concentrated resettlement in multi-storied buildings, the policy of capital investment in the countryside is one of the necessary conditions laid down by local governments for developers bidding for land blocks for urban construction.

Although this mode seems applicable from the perspective of economy, its profound impacts on the rural society are also worth noting. First, as farmers move from the rural living environment into multi-storied buildings, the large-scale population concentration will bring about changes in social relations and new challenges to rural governance. Second, as the multi-storied buildings for concentrated resettlement are detached from cultivated land, farmers will have to buy vegetables and other food from the market, in contrast to the previous self-sufficiency lifestyle, and the costs of living are estimated to increase by about 30%, increasing their economic burden. In addition, as the mass labor forces flow from rural areas into the cities, their families, mostly women, children, and the elderly are left behind, aggravating regional aging problem. Finally, the relationship between the state and farmers has changed. Within the framework of the tax reform, the state ceased to levy agricultural taxes. This move was accompanied by a sharp decrease in the sum of appropriations for local governments in rural areas, which is unfavorable for the rural areas confrontin the trend of aging. Farmers' expectations for a nanny-type government will undoubtedly increase financial pressure of local governments there.

From the representative practices in Chengdu, we can see that these policies had at least the following profound influences on the whole country.

First, it still relied on the combination of land, fiscal revenues, and financial capital to promote urbanization. What's more, it freed itself more thoroughly from the influence of industrialization and population concentration than the eastern regions by mainly counting on the driving force provided by local governments.

Under the premise of capital sufficiency and reliability of local governments for rapid investment and credit expansion, land has become the unique constraint on the urbanization model driven by the trinity of land, fiscal revenues and finance. By "urban-rural integration", the constraints on land quotas for urban construction have been effectively lifted in Chengdu. However, it still carries the bearings and thus may be deemed as an intensified and expanded version of the urbanization model implemented in the eastern regions.

Second, land urbanization and urban-rural integration (specifically, concentrated farmer resettlement in multi-storied buildings and capital investment in the countryside) are combined as a result of relevant cultivated land conserving policies, so not only urban residents and landless farmers but also rural residents are included in the land urbanization.

7.3 A Brief Conclusion on the Relationship Between the Central Government and Local Governments

In this subsection, we will draw some conclusions on the relationship between the central government and local governments mostly on the basis of our analysis in this book.

First of all, the relationship between the central government and local governments is the key to our understanding of the behaviors of local governments as well as local economic and social development. Although we cannot deny that it has been developed during their interactions, the basic framework of the relationship between the central government and local governments has far-reaching influences on the behaviors of local governments. According to our analysis, the tax-sharing system, as a key reform restructuring the relationship between the central government and local governments, is of great significance for our understanding of China's current social and economic development model. Characterized by centralized fiscal powers and decentralized responsibilities and duties, this framework has even higher demands and expectations on local governments in terms of the capability of raising funds and covering its expenditures. And this is the key to the understanding land fiscal revenues and urbanization.

Secondly, since the reform and opening-up, the relationship between the central government and local governments has managed to break loose from the dilemma of “chaos upon decentralization or stagnation upon centralization of powers”. On the whole, the trend of “decentralization” has not been altered by the tax-sharing system, for in the long run, the fiscal centralization thereunder will only lead to even more highlighted authority of local governments. Although this might be seemingly contradictory, according to our analysis, the land fiscal revenues obtained under the tax-sharing system have made local governments to be more and more aware of their status as interest subjects and thus resort to various means, such as profit-oriented land/city operations, etc., to expand their financial resources beyond the strict central control. A review of land administration policies from the historical perspective will reveal that the control of the central government over the behaviors of local governments has been ever diminishing. Up till now, its control over land use has been gradually loosened, not to mention the rapidly lessening of interventions with housing pricing and local financing. This trend is expected to continue in view of the current situation.

Finally, factors decisive for the basic relationship between the central government and local governments include not only the “city operations” of local governments ever since the implementation of the tax-sharing system, but also unconscious promotive role played by the central government. Since the reform and opening up, “economic growth” has always been put in the first place in our ideology led by the central government. And the reform and opening up was essentially centered on “economic growth”. Since the beginning of the 21st Century, regardless of the “Scientific Outlook on Development” stressing economic structural transformation, the tendency of putting more emphasis on economic development instead of society and focusing on material wealth rather than morality has continued and exacerbated, embodying the profit-oriented concept of managing state affairs. Under the guidance of this concept, the central government and local governments will probably keep detaching from each other.

Erratum to: Relationship between the Central Government and Local Governments of Contemporary China

Erratum to:
F. Zhou and M. Tan, *Relationship between the Central Government and Local Governments of Contemporary China*, Social Development Experiences in China,
https://doi.org/10.1007/978-981-10-4388-8

In the original version of the book, the co-publisher name "Science Press" has been changed as "China Social Sciences Press" in the Copyright page of Frontmatter.

The updated online version of this book can be found at
https://doi.org/10.1007/978-981-10-4388-8

F. Zhou and M. Tan, *Relationship between the Central Government and Local Governments of Contemporary China*, Social Development Experiences in China,
https://doi.org/10.1007/978-981-10-4388-8_8

References

Arellano, M., and O. Bover. 1995. Another Look at the Instrumental Variables Estimation of Error Components Models. *Journal of Econometrics* 68: 29–51.

Arellano, M., and S. Bond. 1991. Some Tests of Specification for Panel Data: Monte Carlo Evidence and an Application to Employment Equations. *Review of Economic Studies* 58: 277–297.

Bardhan, Pranab. 2000. Irrigation and Cooperation: An Empirical Analysis of 48 Irrigation Communities in South India. *Economic Development and Cultural Change* 48 (4): 847–865.

Blundell, R., and S. Bond. 1998. Initial Conditions and Moment Restrictions in Dynamic Panel Data Models. *Journal of Econometrics* 87: 11–143.

Bond, S. 2002. Dynamic Panel Data Models: A Guide to Micro Data Methods and Practice. Institute for Fiscal Studies Working Paper 09/02. London: Institute for Fiscal Studies.

Bowsher, C.G. 2002. On Testing Over identifying Restrictions in Dynamic Panel Data Models. *Economics Letters* 77: 211–220.

Buchanan, James M., and Richard A. Musgrave. 2000. *Public Finance and Public Choice: Two Contrasting Visions of the State*. Translated by Lei Chengyao. Beijing: China Financial & Economic Publishing House.

Chen, Xiwen. 2010. Three Major Problems with the Rural Reform. *China Reform* 10.

Chen, Yongfu. 2007. Land Consolidation: Practices and Achievements in Jinyun County. Report by the Development and Reform Bureau of Jinyun County. *Zhejiang Economy* 12.

China Society of Materials Economics, ed. 1983. *History of the Socialist Materials Administration System in China*, 91–92. Beijing: China Logistics Publishing House.

Comprehensive Planning Department of the Ministry of Finance, ed. 1992. *Financial Statistics of China*. Beijing: China Science Publishing & Media Ltd.

Davoodi, Hamid, and Heng-Fu Zou. 1998. Fiscal Decentralization and Economic Growth: A Cross Country Study. *Journal of Urban Economics* 43: 244–423.

De Mello, L.R. 2000. Fiscal Decentralization and Intergovernmental Fiscal Relations: A Cross Country Analysis. *World Development* 28 (2): 365–380.

Dong, Yanbing. 2006. Study on Index Conversion Policies for Rural Land Consolidation in China. *Study on Land Issues in the Process of Establishing Socialist New Countryside*. November 2006. Conference paper.

Eakin, Holtz D., W. Newey, and H.S. Rosen. 1988. Estimating Vector Autoregressions with Panel Data. *Econometrica* 56: 1371–1395.

Editoral Office of Contemporary China Series. 1984. *Reform of the Economic System in Contemporary China*. Beijing: China Social Sciences Press.

Feng, Qiaobin. 2010. Re-recognizing the Huge Debts of Local Government-run Investment & Financing Enterprises in China. *West Forum* 3.

Galasso, Emanuela, and Martin Ravallion. 2001. Decentralization Targeting of an Anti Poverty Program. Mimeo. Development Research Group,World Bank.

F. Zhou and M. Tan, *Relationship between the Central Government and Local Governments of Contemporary China*, Social Development Experiences in China,
DOI 10.1007/978-981-10-4388-8

Gugerty, Mary Kay, and Edward Migual. 2000. *Community Participation and Social Sanctions in Kenyan Schools Mimeo*. Harvard University.

Hansen, L. 1982. Large Sample Properties of Generalized Method of Moments Estimators. *Econometrica* 50 (3): 1029–1054.

Hu, Chuanjing. 2011. Thoughts on Pilot Regulation for Linking the Increase in Land Used for Urban Construction and the Decrease in Land Used for Rural Construction. *Land & Resources* 7.

Huang, Peihua. 2003. *China: National Development and Local Finance*. Beijing: CITIC Press.

Huang, Xiaohu. 2009. Several Opinions on the Circulation of the Contractual Right of Land. *Red Flag Manuscript*, February 2009.

Huang, Xiaowei. 2003. Survey and Thoughts on Rural Land Consolidation in Cangnan County, Zhejiang Province. *Land Consolidation & Urbanization*. Conference paper.

Jiang, Xingsan, Liu Shouying, and Li Qing. 2010. *Land System Reform in China: Policy Evolution & Local Implementation*. Shanghai: Sdx Joint Publishing Company.

Kornai, Janos. 1986. *Economics of Shortage*. Translated by Zhang Xiaoguang et al. Beijing: Economic Science Press.

Li, Hua, Yang Weiqing, and Jiang Guoqiang. 2002. Benifiting the State, the People, and the Collective: A Report on Land Consolidation in Shaoxing County, Zhejiang Province. *China Land*, April 2002.

Li, Xiangyi. 2003. A Study of the Balance of Cultivated Land Occupation and Compensation. *China Land Sciences*, February 2003.

Lin, JustinYifu, and Liu Zhiqiang. Fiscal Decentralization and Economic Growth in China. 2000. CCER. NOC2000008.

Lin, JustinYifu, and Liu Zhiqiang. 2000. Fiscal Decentralization and Economic Growth in China. *Economic Development and Cultural Change* 49 (1): 1–21.

Litvack, J., J. Ahmad, and R. Bird. 1998. *Rethinking Decentralization*. Washington: World Bank.

Liu, Runqiu. 2010. Risks in the Operation of the Cultivated Land Balance Mode and Prevention Measures. *Journal of Sichuan University* 168.

Liu, Shouying, and Jiang Xingsan. 2005. Land Finance & Fiscal/Financial Risks—A Case from a Developed Area in East China. *China Land Sciences* 6.

Liu, Shouying, and Shao Ting. 2013. Unsustainability of the Land Selling Paradigm and Suggestions on Reform. *Internal Research Report of the Development Research Center under the State Council*. Unpublished paper.

Liu, Shouying, Zhou Feizhou, and Shao Ting. 2012. *Land System and Economic Growth in China*. Beijing: China Development Press.

Oates, Wallace E. 1972. *Fiscal Federalism*. New York: Harcourt Brace Jovanovich.

Oi, Jean C. 1992. Fical Reform and the Economic Foundations of Local State Corporatism in China. *World Politics* 45 (1): 99–126.

Qian, Yingyi. 1994. A Theory of Shortage in Socialist Economies based on the 'Soft Budget Constraint'. *American Economic Review* 84 (1): 145–156.

Qian, Yingyi. 2003. How Reform Worked in China. *In Search of Prosperity: Analytic Narratives on Economic Growth*, ed. Dani Rodrik, 297–333. Princeton, NJ: Princeton University Press.

Qian, Yingyi, and Barry R. Weingast. 1996. China's Transition to Markets: Market Preserving Federalism, Chinese Style. *Journal of Policy Reform*. 1 (2): 149–185.

Qian, Yingyi, and Barry R. Weingast. 1997. Federalism As a Commitment to Preserving Market Incentives. *Journal of Economic Perspectives* 11 (4): 83–92.

Qian, Yingyi, and Gerard Roland. 1998. Federalism and the Soft Budget Constrain. *American Economic Review* 88 (5): 1143–1162.

Qian, Yingyi, and Xu Chenggang. 1993. Why China's Economic Reform Differ: The M-form Hierarchy and Entry/Expansion of the Non-state Sector. *Economics of Transition* 1 (2): 135–170.

Qu, Jingdong. 2012. Project Scheme: A New State Administration System. *Social Sciences in China* 5.

Qu, Jingdong, Zhou Feizhou, and Ying Xing. 2009. From Overall Control to Technical Administration. *Social Sciences in China* 6.

Research Group of the Department of Sociology at Tsinghua University. 2011. An Investigation Report on Concentrated Farmers Resettlement in Qingbaijiang District, Chengdu City, Sichuan Province. Unpublished paper.

Rodden, Jonathan, Gunnar S. Eskeland, and Jennie Litvack (eds.). 2003. *Fiscal Decentralization and the Challenge of Hard Budget Constraints*. Cambridge: The MIT Press.

Sargan, J. 1958. The Estimation of Economic Relationships Using Instrumental Variables. *Econometrica* 26 (3): 393–415.

She, Xiaoye, and Chen Yingying. 2011. Hierarchical Operation Mechanism and Governance Logic of the Project Scheme. *Social Sciences in China* 4.

Sun, Liping. 2012. *Institute of Social Advancement, Kaifeng Development Academy and Social Development Seminar, Department of Sociology, Tsinghua University: An Annual Research Report of Social Progress in 2011*. http://news.tsinghua.edu.cn.

Sun, Xiulin, and Zhou Feizhou. 2013. Land Fiscal Revenues and the Tax-sharing System: An Empirical Demonstration. *Social Sciences in China* 3.

Tan, Mingzhi. 2014. Synchronism of a Strict Control and Stimulation: A Review of the Policy of connecting the Increase in Land Used for Urban Construction with the Decrease in Land Used for Rural Construction and Local Implementation. *Social Sciences in China* 7.

Tiebout, Charles M. 1956. A Pure Theory of Local Expenditures. *Journal of Political Economy*. 64 (5): 416–424.

Wang, Hui, and Tao Ran. 2009. On the 'Zhejiang Paradigm' in the Transfer and Transactions of Land Development Rights: Origin of the System, Operation Mode and Its Significance. *Management World* 8.

Wang, Qingri. 2012. An analysis of the land target trade system in Chongqing. *The Blue Book for Land Policies of China*. Beijing: China Social Sciences Press.

Wang, Shaoguang. 1997. *The Threshold of Decentralization*. Beijing: China Planning Press.

Wang, Songlin. 2005. Make New Contributions to the Sustainable Social and Economic Development of Zhejiang Province by Intensifying Land Consolidation and Development. *Zhejiang Land Resources* 10.

Xiang, Huaicheng (ed.). 1994. *Fiscal System Reform in China*. Beijing: China Financial & Economic Publishing House.

Yan, Kun, and Zhang Licheng. 2003. An Analysis of the Financial Difficulties at the Township/County Level in China and Suggestions on Countermeasures. *Review of Economic Research* 90.

Ying, Xing. 2001. *A Story about the River Home Hydropower Station Petitioning Immigrants: From "Asking for an Explanation" to "Restoring Order"*. Beijing: SDX Joint Publishing Company.

Zhang, Tao, and Zou Hengfu. 1998. Fiscal Decentralization, Public Spending, and Economic Growth in China. *Journal of Public Economics* 67 (2): 221–240.

Zhang, Wuchang. 2009. *Economic System of China*. Beijing: CITIC Press.

Zhang, Yan, and Gong Liutang. 2005. Reform of the Tax-sharing System, Fiscal Decentralization and China's Economic Growth. *Economics* (Quarterly) 1.5.

Zhang, Yongsheng. 2009. Relationship between the Central Government and Local Governments: A Theoretical Framework and Its Applications. *Comparative Economic & Social Systems* 142. 2.

Zhang, Yubao. 2004. On Gains and Losses in Balancing Cultivated Land Occupation and Ompensation. *China Land*, December 2004.

Zhao, Yujin. 2011. Policy Logic and Unexpected Results of the Rural Reform in Qingbaijiang District, Chengdu City, Sichuan Province. MA thesis. Department of Sociology, Peking University.

Zheng, Yongnian, and Wu Guoguang. 1995. *On the Relationship between the Central Government and Local Governments: A Key Issue in China's Institutional Transformation*. Hongkong: Oxford University Press.

Zhong, Yang. 2012. Study of Risk Control for the Land Coupon Transaction System in Municipality of Chongqing. Thesis for the MA Degree, Southwest University.

Zhou, Feizhou. 2006a. A Decade of Implementation: The Tax-sharing System and It Impacts. *Social Sciences in China* 6.

Zhou, Feizhou. 2006b. From an Absorptive Regime to a Suspending One. *Sociological Study* 3.

Zhou, Feizhou. 2007. Having the Knack of Making Money: Government and Farmers in Land Development and Transfer. *Sociological Study* 1.

Zhou, Feizhou. 2009. Championship System. *Sociological Study* 3.

Zhou, Feizhou. 2012. *A Benefit Pursuit: Fiscal Relationship and Behaviours of Local Governments*. Shanghai: SDX Joint Publishing Company.

Zhou, Feizhou, and Zhao Yang. 2003. An Analysis of Rural Public Finance: Township Financial Dilemmas and Their Causes. *China Rural Survey* 4.

Zhou, Li'an. 2004. Stimulation and Cooperation of Government Officials in a Promotion Game. *Economic Research Journal* 6.

Zhou, Li'an. 2007. Study of the Championship Paradigm of the Promotion of Local Officials in China. *Economic Research Journal* 7.

Zhou, Qiren. 2010. Allowing Farmers to Share Land Revenue in the Process of Narrowing the Gap between Urban and Rural Areas. *Newsletter about Work in Rural Areas*, October 2010.

Zhou, Qiren, and Comprehensive Research Group of State Development Studies at Peking University. 2010. *Right Returning and Capability Empowering: A Solid Foundation for Long-term Development*. Beijing: Peking University Press.

Zhou, Xueguang. 2009. Inter-local Government Conspiracy: An Institutional Logic of Governmental Behaviors. *Open Society* 12.

Zhou, Xueguang. 2011. Authoritative System and Effective Governance: Institutional Logic of State Administration in Contemporary China. *Open Society* 10.

The manufacturer's authorised representative in the EU is Springer Nature Customer Service Centre GmbH, Europaplatz 3, 69115 Heidelberg, Germany. If you have any concerns regarding our products, please contact ProductSafety@springernature.com

Printed and bound by CPI Group (UK) Ltd, Croydon, CR0 4YY
25/09/2026
02222896-0019